Scribe Publications
DAMO'S BEDSIDE GUIDE
TO THE WORLD CUP

Damien Lovelock is probably best known as the
singer and songwriter for The Celibate Rifles;
however, he has also been covering football, as a
freelancer, for over twenty-five years for JJJ, Vega
FM, SEN Sports Radio, ABC Radio and TV, and
most notably SBS TV's *The World Game,* where
he brings a unique and often hilarious perspective
on the beautiful game. His writing has appeared
in *Inside Sport, Soccer Australia, Rolling Stone,* the
Sydney Morning Herald, and *The Age,* and he is the
author of *Soccer: Great Moments, Great Matches.*
He lives in Sydney.

For
William Lovelock
Joan Lovelock
Luke Lovelock

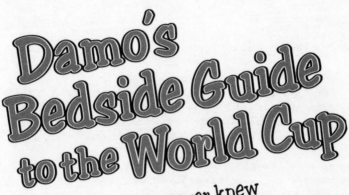

Damo's Bedside Guide to the World Cup

Everything you never knew you needed to know

DAMIEN LOVELOCK

SCRIBE

Melbourne

Scribe Publications Pty Ltd
PO Box 523
Carlton North, Victoria, Australia 3054
Email: info@scribepub.com.au

First published by Scribe 2006

Text design and typesetting by Pauline Haas
Cover design by Darian Causby, Highway 51
Printed and bound in Australia by Griffin Press

National Library of Australia
Cataloguing-in-Publication data

Lovelock, Damien.
Damo's bedside guide to the World Cup.
    ISBN 1 920769 89 7.
    1. Socceroos (Team). 2. World Cup (Soccer).
    3. Soccer. 4. Soccer – Australia. I. Title.
796.334668

www.scribepub.com.au

CONTENTS

Preface

In 1968, through an expression of mutual consent, I changed schools and came into contact with football (or soccer, as we called it then) for the first time. My grandpa, who was unfathomably old, had played for Woolwich Arsenal Gunners in England in the 1890s and early 1900s and a cousin had taken me to a match when I was six. These moments aside, I had never been exposed to soccer — aka wog-ball — in any meaningful way. I had been an A grade rugby union and league player for my entire sporting life, and happily so. My friends were the same.

My first day at the new school, I made several new friends, from Polish, Hungarian, and Greek backgrounds, who were football fans one and all. When autumn came I finally succumbed to my curiosity and agreed to play goalkeeper in the under 15B team, for one game. By half-time I was hooked. We lost 1–0 and I won man-of-the-match.

England was basking in the glory of its 1966 World Cup triumph and all the guys at school followed one of the English teams, be it Manchester United with George Best and Bobby Charlton, Leeds with Bremner and Lorimer, or Chelsea with Osgood and Harris to name but a few. Every Monday night we watched Match of the Day from the BBC. Sometimes they showed the Home Internationals featuring England, Scotland, Wales and Northern Ireland. In Sydney we went to the Sports Ground to see teams like Moscow Dynamo, Manchester City, and AS Roma play against NSW. I found the mixture of cultures, accents, and languages absolutely intoxicating.

Then in 1970 my life changed forever when I experienced my first World Cup and the joys of Pele's Brazil, Booby Moore's England, Beckenbauer's Germany, and Facchetti's Italy. We followed it in the newspapers, on the radio, and on TV — a snippet here, a fragment there. We discussed, imagined, and debated the results of matches we had never seen. I listened to the final, broadcast in Portuguese, on a crystal set. And then it was over — for four years. I thought I'd die.

This, then, is a subjective account of my love affair with the world game and its pinnacle, the World Cup — not just a football tournament but a carnival of cultures and a celebration of life itself. I hope you enjoy it.

I'd like to thank John Hunter from Scribe; Les Murray, Craig Foster, Jorge Lazo, Simon Hill, Andrew Orsatti, and Tony Palumbo from SBS; and Kate Gill from the Matildas.

Also thanks to Patrik and Margo Pollnow, Alex Walton, Lee Matthews, Lucy Kemp, Margaret Edgar, Kevin Long, Pommy Mick, Damo from Carlito's, Rocket, and the high cost of living.

Finally, thank-you to John Logie Baird, Mexico 1970, Johann Cruyff and Holland 1974, Matt le Tissier, Belgium 1986, Italy 1982 and Cesare Maldini.

The curse of the Socceroos

Many lives, Arjuna, you and I have lived.
I remember them all, but thou dost not.
— Bhagavad-gita, iv, 5

'I don't believe in an interventionist God', sang Nick Cave in 'Into My Arms'. This makes one thing about Nick Cave perfectly clear: he is not now, nor has he ever been, a supporter of the Socceroos. For if ever there was a team that prompted its faithful followers to look to the realm of the metaphysical for answers, it's the Australian football team. I'm not talking about a single, conclusive phenomenon, like statues that cry or relics that levitate. Rather it's a series of foully unjust events that have collectively cursed every campaign from the early seventies to 2005. Since qualifying for the 1974 World Cup finals (our solitary appearance at the greatest show on Earth), we have contrived to avoid a repeat appearance no less than seven times, and in a variety of circumstances that mere causal logic or Newtonian physics cannot adequately explain.

In that time Australian soccer has been in exile, lost on a vexed journey of self-discovery that has assumed the increasingly desperate qualities of some weird, epic endurance event strung out over thirty years and five continents. Three decades of disaster, betrayal, failure, and sheer bad luck that were finally put to rest when John Aloisi slotted home the winning penalty to eliminate Uruguay and send us on our way to Germany 2006. Somewhere along the line you've got to ask yourself: 'What did we ever do to deserve this?' Like so many tales that assume mythic proportions, the truth behind the curse of the Socceroos is a simple, if an unnaturally strange story. It begins back at our first World Cup campaign in Phnom Penh in 1965. The man we have to blame for our trail of tears is former Australian Soccer Federation honcho Jim Bayutti, who finally convinced all parties to take the plunge and try our luck at the 1966 tournament being held in England. As Oceania representatives we were lumped in with the best teams from Asia and Africa to play-off for one place in the finals. When this was announced most African nations withdrew in protest, arguing that the African federation should be guaranteed a spot in the final sixteen. The Asians thought likewise and before you could say 'mass exodus' the group representing three continents had been reduced to two nations: Australia and the mysterious North Korea.

The two qualification matches were played in neutral Phnom Penh in November 1965 with a three day break between matches. Australian spirits were high and a general feeling of optimism was all pervasive — and why not, after all, who had ever heard of North Korea? The Aussies learnt all they needed to know about their opponents very abruptly when the first game finished 6–1 in favour of the 'football nobodies' and the dream was well and truly over when they cleaned up the Socceroos again, 3–1, in the second. The Anglo-Aussie soccer press pronounced it a disaster and we were warned to 'stop fooling around with the World Cup' by London based soccer scribe Eric Batty. The North Koreans went on to enjoy a brief, but brilliant, cameo in the limelight at the 1966 finals, eliminating Italy 1–0 and leading Portugal 3–0 before being run down by a rampaging Eusebio. Then, as mysteriously as they had arrived, they disappeared into the mists of time never to be seen again at this level, thanks to a wild combination of boycotts, withdrawals, and failed attempts to qualify.

Undaunted, preparations began immediately for the 1970 World Cup being held in Mexico, and Australian tours by Scotland, Greece, and Japan were just part of the Socceroos' build-up to the 1969 qualifiers. Official qualification began in earnest in Seoul on October 10, 1969 where we met Japan who, without their brilliant centre-forward Kamamoto, we accounted for 3–1. We then beat the hosts, South Korea, 2–1, leaving the pitch under a hailstorm of bottles, cushions, and fruit. Two draws from return matches against the Japanese and South Koreans over the next ten days were enough for us to win that qualification group and go on to meet Rhodesia in Laurenco Marques. Surely this would be just another mere formality before the globetrotting Aussies went on to meet Israel for a place at the big show.

It was around about now that things started to get weird. The two 'mere formality' matches against Rhodesia ended in 1–1 and 0–0 draws, requiring an unscripted third match to break the deadlock. Our problems were threefold: one, the referee seemed to be under instructions to allow the home side to kick us to death, and getting into the spirit, they attempted to do so with unbridled enthusiasm; two, Rhodesia's beanpole goalkeeper Robin Jordan, who looked as though he couldn't catch a cold in an Antarctic blizzard, had nonetheless proved to be a hero for the locals; and three, we had no time to waste as we had to beat the Rhodesians and then get to Israel within the week for the first leg of the play-off for a place in Mexico.

Panic set in after the second draw. In a moment of mephistophelian inspiration, Australian liaison officer Fernando Fernandes, whose office was contained within the best cat-house in Laurenco Marques, contacted the most powerful witchdoctor in the country. In return for the princely sum of £50 he offered to place a curse on the Rhodesian goalkeeper. The Australians quickly agreed and lost no time in relaying this information to their opponents. Sure enough, in the third and deciding match, the keeper had a shocker and we aced the game 3–1. Israel, here we come. After a night of victory celebrations, the team assembled at the airport the next day to fly to Tel Aviv when suddenly the

witchdoctor appeared. In an unfortunate oversight it seemed he
had not been paid. The team manager, still recovering from a vig-
orous night on the turps, refused to honour the Socceroo's debt.
The witchdoctor calmly replied that he could just as easily place a
curse on the aeroplane and all those in it. But the team manager
remained unmoved ... and so did the curse, for over thirty years.
The Aussies left Rhodesia with the debt unpaid and flew to Israel,
losing 1–0 in Tel Aviv four days later, then reconvened in Sydney
after a fortnight, where a 1–1 draw was the best we could manage.
Israel went to Mexico and we went back to the drawing board to
prepare for the 1974 campaign.

Over the next three years the Socceroos played Iran, Greece,
Israel, Mexico, South Vietnam, Indonesia, South Korea, the
Philippines, and Bulgaria in preparation for the elimination round.
Our qualifying group got under way in Auckland on March 4,
1973 with a 1–1 draw against New Zealand. We followed this
with victories over Iraq and Indonesia and another draw with
New Zealand. With coach Rale Rasic at the helm things were
starting to look good: a nil all draw with Iraq and a 6–0 thumping
of Indonesia, with goals to Mackay, Atti Abonyi (2), Richards, and
the great Ray Baartz, gave us victory in our sub-group and placed
us in the box seat. Next up we met Iran in Sydney and stitched
them up neatly 3–0: we were almost there. The return leg in
Tehran resulted in a 2–0 triumph for the home team; we lost the
battle but had won the war 3–2 on aggregate.

Australia's final hurdle to qualify for the 1974 World Cup
would be South Korea. The two teams met for the first leg before
a capacity crowd at the Sydney Sports Ground on October 28,
1973 where they fought out a nil all draw — the Aussie's inability
to score, let alone win, at home was something we would see
repeated for the next 28 years. The re-match was in Seoul on
November 10 and we got off to a fabulous start, falling behind 2–0

inside the first thirty minutes. But even as the Korean cheers for the second goal were still ringing in the stadium, Col Curran got away down the flank and crossed to Branko Buljevic, who headed home to give Australia a lifeline. Just two minutes into the second half, a Ray Baartz bomb tied the game at 2–2 and that was the way it finished, requiring a third, deciding match to be played in neutral Hong Kong three days later.

Although both games had been drawn, the pendulum had definitely begun to swing Australia's way. Blowing a 2–0 lead at home had damaged the Korean's morale and self-belief, whereas we'd got ourselves out of jail and we weren't about to go back for our hats. For the first sixty minutes in Hong Kong the Socceroos played their best football and dominated, but the elusive goal would not come. Then, twenty minutes before full time, midfielder Jimmy McKay picked up a loose ball thirty yards from the Korean goal and hammered home a thunderbolt to clinch victory and a place at the 1974 World Cup finals.

> *All Hail*
> *The Holy Grail*
> *And Jimmy McKay*
> *Who did not fail.* (Anon)

History shows that Australia took its place at the tournament in West Germany in Group One, alongside Chile and East and West Germany, returning home with a 2–0 and 3–0 loss to the respective Germans and a nil all draw with Chile. Upon returning, preparations began immediately for our inevitable return to the big show in four years time in Argentina. For the Aussies had made the big-time, the Socceroo juggernaut was rolling and nothing would stop it now: certainly not some ludicrous curse placed on the team by some ridiculous witchdoctor at some long-forgotten airfield in Mozambique.

Following the Socceroos' 1974 triumph in reaching the finals, the Australian Soccer Federation (ASF) responded by sacking the coach, Rale Rasic. The reasons for this were never made clear. Rasic was succeeded by an Englishman, Brian Green, who began well but suddenly resigned and flew back to England following a match at the MCG in which Australia defeated New Zealand 3–1. The official explanation was contained in a curt press release which announced that Green had been arrested for shoplifting. A ballot was hastily arranged to fill the vacant position. Again successful coach Rasic was overlooked, as was another eminently logical choice, the former Socceroo captain Johnny Warren. Instead, the ASF chose Jim Shoulder, another Englishman about whom virtually nothing was known. Australia was eliminated from the 1978 finals after home and away losses to both Iran and Kuwait. The players and the media placed a large portion of the blame squarely on the shoulders of Shoulder. The ASF's response? Retain him as national coach immediately.

Perhaps an appropriate motto for the ASF would have been 'confused in victory, magnanimous in defeat'. Yet a little over a year later, Shoulder was dumped and replaced by the West German Rudi Gutendorf, again without adequate explanation. All that was known about Gutendorf was that he had been recommended to the ASF by the world governing body, FIFA. Immediately he set about guiding the Socceroos' campaign for qualification in Spain in 1982. Between 1979 and 1981, Australia defeated Taiwan and Israel and drew with Czechoslovakia, Northern Ireland, Mexico and Greece. The signs were very good, but when the World Cup campaign began, the Darkness descended. Herr Gutendorf crowned his period as national coach with a 3–3 draw against New Zealand in Auckland in the first leg — a game in which the Socceroos lead three times — followed by a 2–0 loss to the All Whites in the return leg in Sydney. Okay, upsets happen — but the

Socceroos conceding five goals in two matches to New Zealand is like Australia losing a Test match to Greenland by an innings. Following the second leg loss, Gutendorf was quoted as saying: 'Australia still has a chance to qualify'. Yeah right ... and Harold Holt will re-surface and be back on dry land any day now.

Following Gutendorf's departure came the appointment of Frank Arok. Beginning as a caretaker for the caretaker (Les Scheinflug, who was overseas at the time), Arok quickly established himself as a popular figure with both players and officials — something Gutendorf had demonstrably failed to do. With his sights set firmly on Mexico 1986, Arok began the process of sifting through the post-Rudi rubble to rebuild a team. It was with a tangible and growing sense of optimism that the Socceroos approached their qualifying round against New Zealand, Israel, and Chinese Taipei. Beginning in their usual World Cup style, with a guns-a-blazing nil-all draw in Auckland, our boys then defeated Israel away, drew with them at home, destroyed Chinese Taipei in both matches and then caned those pesky New Zealanders 2–0. Normally this would have been the signal for mass celebration among devotees across the land, but in this case, no. Because, in a demonstration of their total lack of commitment to the development of the world game in the Oceania region, FIFA had added two final qualifying matches against the runners-up in European Group Seven. What had we done to deserve this cruel twist? Nothing — except that otherwise it would've been too easy, wouldn't it?

And so it was that we headed off for another rendezvous with fate in the form of Scotland at Hampden Park. The Scots, full-time professionals to a man, triumphed 2–0 over the gallant Socceroos and their coach 'Mad Dog Arok', as the Scottish media endearingly dubbed him. In a scene that would become all too familiar in the next decade, Australia, in the return leg at the MCG, battled valiantly and sometimes brilliantly, but could only manage a 0–0 draw. And so our most successful campaign since '74 came to nought thanks to the addition of a new qualifying criterion which seemed to defy logic.

Surely now the pattern is starting to emerge: forces beyond the ordinary physical plane were at work to thwart the Socceroos at every turn. Still, they pushed on in their quest for glory, blind to the fact that fate was conspiring to manufacture their doom in a never-ending variety of colours and flavours. Arok was retained as head honcho as the Socceroos set sail for Italy 1990. Again the usual suspects were assembled, again the Aussies came out firing, and again they went down 2–0 in Auckland. They were nothing if not consistent. But they recovered from that setback, and the subsequent 1–1 result in Tel Aviv — with defender Charlie Yankos putting in a direct free kick from 50 metres out which must rank as one of the greatest individual efforts of all time — was achieved in such a manner that great optimism was re-kindled among the faithful.

And so we trooped to the newly erected Sydney Football Stadium to witness the Socceroos rampant in victory. Our lads launched wave after wave of attack, but alas, no goal was forthcoming. Then, with ten minutes remaining Israel scored following a mix up between Socceroo defenders Yankos and Van Egmond, which allowed Israeli striker Ohana to swoop on the loose ball. Turning to chase back, Yankos stumbled giving Ohana the priceless headstart that he needed: 1–0 to Israel. The Socceroos clawed one back and had their opposition on the ropes, but the referee inexplicably ended the match six minutes early. Despite coach Arok and Socceroo Oscar Crino's best efforts, the blundering referee survived and left Australia alive. Would a microscopic examination of the playing surface have revealed the cause of Charlie's sudden loss of footing? Could the most skilful Swiss watchmaker detect the flaw in the referee's match-timing device

that robbed us of impending victory? No, for the hands that prac-
tised such malevolent magic are clearly not of this world.

The heartbroken Frank Arok stepped aside, handing the
coaching mantle to Eddie Thomson. Again, the Socceroos rose to
embrace their long-awaited date with destiny at USA '94, and
again the signs were good: new players, new tactics, and a new
beginning. Again, FIFA rose to the occasion and gave us a brand
new friend to play with — Argentina! World Champions in '86,
runners-up in '90! Thanks a bunch, guys. And just to top it off,
Diego Maradona decided to come out of retirement for the two
qualifying matches.

In Sydney, the Aussies played Argentina into the ground but
could only draw 1–1. In the return leg they lost 1–0 after an own
goal from Socceroo captain Alex Tobin. Again the bewildered fans
could sense the unseen world at work, for which two players
would have been voted the most reliable in their respective teams
— the two least likely to hand a match to their opponents? Charlie
Yankos and Alex Tobin.

Following the tragedy of World Cup '94, Eddie Thomson
resigned and headed to Japan. David Hill, boss of Soccer Australia,
promptly secured the coaching services of none other than former
England mentor Terry Venables. His brief was simple: France '98,
the World Cup or bust. In contrast to previous campaigns,
Venables was given more than a hearty handshake and some fre-
quent flier points to go with his ambitious assignment, in fact, he
virtually scored an open cheque book. And so here's how it all
goes down . . .

The Socceroos waltz through the qualifiers and win the
Oceania zone. Then come friendlies against Macedonia, Hungary
and Tunisia and we win them all. Finally, we learn that our opponent will be none other than Iran, back from a twenty-year
self-imposed exile — why couldn't it have been twenty-one,

haven't these guys heard of numerology? Johnny Warren warns us that Iran is one of the best teams in Asia. No matter — they've got the arse out of their pants, we'll kill 'em. This is OUR time. So the Aussies head for Tehran. Half our team hasn't played any football for months and are wearing name tags to get to know each other at the last practice session in Dubai: 'Hi, my name's Harry, I play left wing'. We play poorly but defend well, pulling off a 1–1 draw. Now we know we've got 'em. This is the team that has played great and lost for twenty years. It seems as if the karmic worm has turned.

We return to Melbourne for the return leg, where the MCG looks more like a set for 'Lord of the Dance' than a sudden-death World Cup qualifier. The nouveau 'fans' love it. They watch intently as the teams warm up, drinking it all in, but the older heads are looking skyward. Surely nothing can go wrong now. The god of football couldn't have any nasty tricks left, and if he has, surely it's someone else's turn: go and pick on Brazil, they can afford it.

The match begins and it's like the Socceroos are playing to 'The Ride of the Valkyries' while Iran are stuck with a Donny and Marie Osmond cassette that's so old it won't play at the right speed. As Johnny Warren later observed: 'If it was a fight, you'd have stopped it after ten minutes.' The Socceroos dominate the Iranians but somehow contrive to lead only 1–0 at half-time, courtesy of Harry Kewell slotting home a cross that had eluded the disorganised Iranian defence. The second half begins where the first ended, with the Aussies so superior they seem irresistible and within three minutes the second goal comes. 2–0, as Aurelio Vidmar cleans up a header that had rebounded off the crossbar: we're going to France, no doubt about it. I'm sitting amongst the Iranian print journalists and they can barely bring themselves to watch: a third goal can only be minutes away and then the party will begin.

But the Other World is nothing if not resourceful. So you think you've seen it all: holes in the ground that open up to trap unwitting defenders, own goals from impossible angles, defeat by New Zealand? Think again, brother. From out of the crowd comes serial pest, Peter Hoare, who's spent thirty-odd years rehearsing for the moment. Unseen by virtually everyone, including a sizable police and security contingent, he races across the field and tears down the net. No big deal, just a short delay for running repairs. The new fans continue to party. The players, coaches and officials look dumbfounded or bemused. But for the older heads in the crowd this was the first sign that things were about to get weird: reach for the Prozac, silver bullets, holy water, cloves of garlic, prayer wheels ... whatever. They sense what's coming because they've seen it all before. The hand of fate is upon them, the Darkness is creeping in ...

Six minutes later the game gets going again, but the atmosphere is no longer celebratory: it's surreal. Iran grabs the flimsy lifeline like any drowning man would, and in the time it takes to eat an MCG hot dog, the dream is over. 1996 Asian Player of the Year Khodadad Azizi creates the first goal for team mate Bagheri and then knocks in the second himself after a delightful through ball from the grand old man of Persian football, Ali Daie. It's 2–2, and that's good enough for the Iranians. The Socceroos fight desperately for a third goal, a goal they so obviously deserve, a goal they have earned ten times over in this match. But we know that it's not going to happen. It's fate, and that's all there is to it.

The impact of the Iran game at the MCG was tsunami-like. I know people who will tell you that they've never quite gotten over that terrible evening's events. I know because I'm one of them. Johnny Warren, weeping on television unable to find the words to complete his match summary, spoke for all of us. In the fallout from the disaster, first Venables and then David Hill resigned leaving an administration that was gutted in every sense. The vacuum at the heart of it was the absence of a coach which, despite the best efforts of Raul Blanco, wasn't properly filled until August 1999 when former Socceroo player Frank Farina was appointed. While lacking the pedigree of previous coaches, Farina had had an impressive playing career in Europe and a short but successful stint as coach in the National Soccer League.

A squad was assembled, preliminary matches were arranged (against everyone from the Cook Islands through to Manchester United), and Oceania group qualifiers were played and won, producing score-lines like 22–0 against Tonga and 31–0 against the highly regarded American Samoa. Until finally in November 2001, having again triumphed in Oceania, we faced up to the fifth-placed South American team: Uruguay.

We'd had a bit to do with these guys back in 1974 and it hadn't worked out all that well. Having already qualified, Uruguay appointed a new coach who decided to bring them to Australia to play two warm-up games six weeks before the finals in West Germany. The first match was played in Melbourne and resulted in a 0–0 draw. It was a rough match with the Aussies refusing to be pushed around. Frustrated by the draw, the Uruguayans promised a better showing in the second game in Sydney. Round two was played on April 27, 1974 and remains etched in Socceroo folklore. In an absolutely vicious game, Australia achieved perhaps their greatest ever victory with a 2–0 win over a nation that had twice won the World Cup. Such was the enormity of the result, that United Press International checked the final score seven times before putting it on the wire overseas. But for Australia, the victory was almost overshadowed by a truly horrific injury to Socceroo striker Ray Baartz, when he was felled behind play by a karate chop from Uruguayan defender Luis Garisto, which badly damaged his carotid artery and nearly killed him. Baartz was undoubtedly

Australia's best player and the injury caused him to miss the World Cup finals and to never play international football again

The two teams met for a place at the 2002 tournament in Korea/Japan, with the first leg to be played back at the scene of the crime, the MCG. The Uruguayans had some great players in Recoba, Montero, and Forlan but the nouveau fans expected victory nonetheless — who had ever heard of Uruguay? The answer of course was that they were one of the most successful teams in World Cup history but that seemed like ancient history now to the part-time press who installed the Aussies as favourites. When we triumphed, 1–0 thanks to a Kevin Muscat penalty, it seemed like needless pessimism on the part of the Aussie soccer establishment but still, older heads shrugged politely and held their tongues. In the return leg in Montevideo, we faced the kind of ferocious reception for which the hosts are notorious and were torn to pieces on the pitch. Despite Australia having the better of the game early on, the Uruguayans sealed their qualification ruthlessly 3–0; the sight of defender Tony Vidmar weeping as he left the pitch in Montevideo lingers as an icon of Australian sport.

While disappointing, the result was a piece of cake compared to the loss to Iran as we had been thoroughly beaten by a better team and no-one could argue otherwise. The football public now waited for the response from Soccer Australia and it came immediately with a stoic 'steady as she goes'. There was no pressure for a new coach and certainly no suggestion from the incumbent that he might resign, no thought of pursuing other options or alternative strategies — nothing. In fact the only rumbling of action on the Australian soccer front came from FIFA headquarters, when President Sepp Blatter surprised everyone by promising Oceania direct qualification for the next World Cup. However before we'd finished debating the merits of this early Christmas gift the offer was withdrawn. Oh well, easy come, easy go.

It was with this background of uncertainty and discontent within Australian football circles that the campaign for Germany 2006 was begun. The usual local suspects in the Oceania qualification group were gathered together and duly dispatched with little ceremony. Next came friendlies against South Africa, Iraq, and Indonesia, and while the Socceroos came through these unbeaten, the results were unconvincing. The players looked stale and disorganised, the attack seemed to falter whenever it met resistance, and defensively we were a mess. Calls for a change of coach, or at least a clarification of tactics, began to grow in volume and in number but other voices reasoned that these were just friendly matches and besides, we still had the Confederations Cup to get things right.

Meanwhile, a series of unrelated events were unfolding that would change the course of Australian football forever. After years of discontent with consistent international failure and the environment of corruption, factional in-fighting, and general mismanagement within Soccer Australia, pressure from the public and in particular the media finally provoked a response. Of course, it didn't come from within but was forced on Soccer Australia by the Federal Ministry for Sport who initiated an independent enquiry to critically assess the way the game was run in Australia. The results of the investigation, known as the Crawford Report, were announced in April 2003: it was a comprehensive plan to reform and restructure the management of the game at every level. The release of the report finally moved Soccer Australia to action: within days the board had threatened to resign en masse. But when their complaints were brushed aside it became obvious that things were about to change and for once the force of history seemed to be working for the good of football in Australia. In July 2003 it was announced that businessman Frank Lowy would oversee the implementation of the Crawford Report's recommendations. By September a new, interim administrative body called the Australian Soccer Association was announced, with Lowy as chairman, which finally, in January 2005 formally became the Football Federation Australia (FFA). After years of stagnation things were now happening at pace, in February former Rugby Union boss John O'Neil was named as CEO and in August a new, revitalized domestic competition called the A League kicked off. As the revolution gained momentum, the pressure was on at all levels to perform.

Meanwhile, action of a different kind was being taken which was to have perhaps an even more powerful effect on the Socceroos' chances for World Cup qualification. In 2004, Australian TV prankster John Safran was preparing a new comedy-adventure series called *John Safran vs God* which focused on obscure religions around the world. Safran had read about the curse on Australian soccer in former Socceroo captain Johnny Warren's autobiography and, as part of his new show, he travelled to Mozambique to find the witchdoctor and get him to remove the hex. As luck would have it, the original witchdoctor had died, but he was able to find another in Maputo, Mozambique who claimed to be able to channel the dead witchdoctor and so settle the decades-old debt and lift the curse. Personal sacrifice for team glory is the great cliché of sport, but few have sacrificed as much as Safran who, dressed in full Socceroo team kit, was ritually anointed in chicken blood at the site of the fateful game in (what is now) Zimbabwe. He returned to Australia, where he and Johnny Warren, as the representative of the team that had brought down the curse, journeyed to the Sydney Football Stadium and smeared themselves in the witchdoctor's unique medicinal clay to purify the team and so finally lay the curse to rest forever. Believe it or not.

The Confederations Cup in Germany came and went in mid 2005 with Australia failing to win a point: losing to the hosts 4–3, Argentina 3–2, and Tunisia 2–0. On the surface, the first two results look reasonable, but in reality they flattered the mediocre Aussies. Although we had been able to score, when the key matches were up for grabs we were not good enough to break the opposition down, and when they came at us we were a rabble in defence and haemorrhaged goals. And then something happened that was virtually unheard of in the history of football in this country. In response to a string of failures, we sacked the coach — the times they were a changin'.

The replacement appointed by the FFA wasn't bad either, Guus Hiddink, regarded by some as currently the best coach in world football, and who had already been to the World Cup semi-finals twice, with Holland and most recently South Korea. But even for a coach of Hiddink's calibre, this would be no picnic. Appointed as a part-timer due to his commitments with Dutch league side PSV Eindhoven, he would have less than four months to prepare the team for their elimination matches against old enemy Uruguay. And so, after friendlies against the Solomon Islands and Jamaica, the Socceroos set off for the Centenario in Montevideo to meet our nemesis of 2001. In a tense nail-biter we went down 1–0, but two memories from the game lingered to give us hope. Viduka had looked dangerous in attack and had gone very close to scoring but perhaps more profoundly, in the last fifteen minutes of the match, Uruguay had shown a desperation for a second goal that we had not been able to provoke four years earlier. The looks on the faces of the Uruguayans as they left the field in Montevideo with a one goal advantage said it all: they knew it wasn't enough.

The return leg in Sydney, four days later, will live long in the memory of the eighty thousand people who were there and the four million who watched it on TV. The Uruguayans started the better team and with a little luck could have had the game sewn up 2–0, following missed chances to Recoba and Morales. But therein lies the story — for the first time in thirty-two years, luck was with the Socceroos, a point that was reinforced when Tony Popovic was not sent off for a violently clumsy tackle on Recoba that should have earned him a red card. Luck continued to run with the Aussies when in the thirty-fifth minute Harry Kewell mis-hit a ball that fell perfectly for Bresciano in the box, and bang: 1–0 to Australia.

Neither side managed to score again and so, with one home goal each from the two legs, the match went to the dreaded penalty shoot-out. The Socceroos had trained for this moment as recently as the day before the game, in fact, their dress-rehearsal was so thorough that captain Mark Viduka had missed his penalty at training to the same side as he would ultimately miss in the game. The script they had followed at training called for Marco Bresciano to step up to take the third penalty after Harry Kewell and Lucas Neill, but now Bresciano was unavailable as, injured and exhausted, he had been substituted for John Aloisi. With the entire qualification campaign now at stake, the coaching staff needed an understudy for the most invidious role in football. Jason Culina was asked first, but politely declined. Josip Skoko was the next candidate, but as he had only been on the ground for a matter of minutes he pointed out that he hadn't even had a chance to warm-up. Vince Grella said that he would take a penalty, but only after goalkeeper Schwartzer had taken his turn, i.e. when pigs fly.

Into the breach stepped Tony Vidmar. Socceroo assistant coach Graeme Arnold later confessed that he was unable to remember the veteran defender ever taking a penalty before that night, even at training. But if you watch the video of the shoot-out, of the four successful penalties taken by the Socceroos that night, none was more assured or professionally executed than Vidmar's. Certainly none would have felt sweeter than for the man who had left Uruguay's Centenario in tears four years earlier. It would be unfair to Mark Schwarzer to say that the Aussie's new-found luck played a hand in the penalty shoot-out as the Socceroo goalkeeper emerged as the hero of the night with two magnificent penalty saves, but when John Aloisi famously drove home his penalty after successful attempts by Kewell, Neill, and Vidmar the curse of the Socceroos had finally been broken.

As we turn our attention to Germany 2006 with one eye fixed cautiously on the past, the words of William Shakespeare in *Julius Caesar* seem unusually appropriate:

> There is a tide in the affairs of men, which taken at
> the flood, leads on to fortune. Omitted, all the voyage
> of their life is bound in shallows and in miseries. On
> such a full sea are we now afloat. And we must take
> the current when it serves, or lose our ventures.

We've had our share of miseries; now is the time for action that will create our own good fortune. Was there ever really a curse, is it at an end, and did it make any difference anyway? All I know is that John Safran is on my Christmas card list for all eternity.

TACTICS
and
STRATEGY

Football is fundamentally a simple game. To quote the great Johann Cruyff: 'To win you have to score one more goal than your opponent.' Absolutely — but how?

To answer this question we need to think about tactics and strategy. The key is to get a perfect balance between attack and defence. If you have too many players in attack, then you will have an inadequate defence. The reverse is also true — just ask anyone who watched the Sweden versus Brazil semi-final in the 1994 World Cup. To understand the present formations, let's go back to England around 1850 and see what was happening then.

Early days

A football match in the 1850s was like an under-7s game in the local park. Players were strung across the field, with perhaps two of them committed to defence. This was quickly abandoned in favour of something like a Rugby Union rolling maul, where all players move together in the same direction. This game was a bit like trench warfare. Players stood in two lines facing each other, about ten metres apart, and then charged. The major problem with this was that teamwork was virtually impossible, as the players were too close together to pass to each other effectively, and there could be no depth in defence or attack.

The first big development was during the years 1870–80. The Scottish national team began playing England regularly and developed the revolutionary 'pairing and passing' system. It proved to be an overwhelming success because it promoted inter-passing and team play rather than the skills of each individual player. It was simple and effective: the Scottish players moved down the field in twos and, as they came up to the opposition fullback, the one that had the ball would pass to his pair. The first time they tried it the result was a draw. However, in the next fifteen years England managed only one victory and suffered defeats of 7–2, 6–1, 5–1. It was a tactical success for Scotland!

In response to this, the English developed the 2–3–5, or Pyramid, system. It was very popular with fans and players alike as it made the game far more open and interesting. It was so successful, in fact, that it was used for the next forty years. There was more space for each player, and greater scope for a 'second phase' or midfield (the three halves) to attack as well as the forwards.

The key player in this formation was the centre-half. He attacked and defended, as did his two midfield team mates, and could choose to pass to the right or left or send a long ball forward. The fullbacks guarded the area in front of the goal.

Midfield Dominance

The next major change in the game was in 1925 and was probably brought in by Herbert Chapman, manager of Arsenal. The 'off-side' rule had been modified so that there only had to be two defenders (for example, the goalkeeper and one other) between an attacker and the goal instead of three. This meant that using the offside trap as a defensive philosophy was far more risky. Chapman's response was to dream up the 'WM' formation.

You can see in the diagram that the centre-half has become a centre-back or stopper, a defender in the middle of the W. His job was to mark the opposing centre-forward. The inside forwards now directed or controlled the attack, which meant that the midfield dominated the game. From now on, virtually all British matches would be won and lost in this crucial area. Because of Herbert Chapman's system, Arsenal dominated League and Cup football for several years, establishing a reputation that survives to this day.

While the WM formation became the standard in Britain, it didn't make it in Europe. The Austrians were using the 2–3–5 system (the old Pyramid) but with one major difference. While the English preferred the more emotional 'Charge of the Light Brigade' approach and used long passes to launch attacks from downfield, the Austrians, Hungarians and Czechs used a short passing game. Their emphasis was on skill and control, and on keeping the ball as close to the ground as possible — 'on the carpet'.

The Italians used a combination of the WM and the 2–3–5 system. At the 1930 World Cup an Italian journalist remarked 'the other team does all the attacking, but Italy wins the game'. This heralded the advent of counter-attacking football: quick, precise, and deadly. The Italians still use it today. But most South American teams continued to favour the 2–3–5 system with the emphasis on attack.

Ever since Herbert Chapman had turned the centre-half into a centre-back the job description for a centre-forward had changed from *'elusive, with good dribbling and heading skills; clean; non-smoker'* to something like *'must be 195 cm, 104 kg (6'6", 16 stone), able to run for 90 minutes; should enjoy physical pain and have very little regard for personal safety'*. In other words, you needed Superman without a cape.

To the dismay of coaches around the world, in the 1950s there were no caped crusaders to be found anywhere. To solve this dilemma, Hungarian coach Gustav Sebes came up with a formation, based around the 'deep-lying centre-forward'. The core of his team structure was Nandor Hidegkuti, who dropped back from the true centre-forward position to play in the midfield as an attacking centre-half. In effect Sebes inverted the 'M' formation and turned it into a 'W' in attack (making WW). The main point of this change was that it caused a headache for the opposition centre-back. If he came forward to mark Hidegkuti in midfield, he left a huge gap in front of goal. If he stayed in position, then Hidegkuti simply cut the opposition to pieces with his passing game.

The Hungarian national team used this formation to great effect in the 1950s, and was virtually unbeatable. They put together a streak of twenty-eight games undefeated — but more of this later.

The strange case of the Swiss bolt

At the same time as Gustav Sebes was perfecting his system, another tactical change was taking place in Uruguay. It was to inspire one of the most exciting periods in world football — the Golden Age of Brazil. But this story begins on the other side of the world in a country better known for chocolate and numbered bank accounts: Switzerland. Now, 'Switzerland' and 'football' are not exactly two words that combine in most people's minds with the force of, say, 'long' and 'weekend'. However, at the 1950 World Cup tournament, an unheard-of system from this little country produced two of the most amazing results in World Cup football. The coach who concocted this miracle in the Alps was Karl Rappan, and his system was called the *verrou*, or Swiss bolt.

The strategy required all ten players to travel all over the field, changing from attack to defence, and vice versa, with alarming speed. The extreme fitness requirements were its biggest problem and, as a result, very few coaches and players were willing to try it. You can see the advanced position of the midfield, especially the centre-half, in attack.

Swiss bolt attack

In defence, the whole team drops back. The 'stopper', or centre-back, goes deep into his own penalty area, sliding back and forth behind the last line of defence, hence the name 'Swiss bolt'. You can see the crowding in front of the goal, with all the free space packed with defenders.

The same approach to football would later resurface in Italy as a system known and dreaded (by fans as much as rival teams) as *catenaccio*.

Before Karl Rappan invented his Swiss bolt everyone still assumed that the number-one requirement for playing high-level football was skill. Tactics like the bolt helped to change all that. Very fit players could play the system even if they weren't as

Swiss bolt defence

skilful, but very skilful players could not play it unless they were also super-fit. And so the emphasis shifted from skill to stamina.

This approach really caught on in Britain. The 1966 World Cup tournament was won by an English side described as courageous, selfless, hard-working, honest … in fact, everything except skilful and intelligent. George Best, possibly the most gifted British player of all time, said:

> 'Stamina's all right, you've got to be able to run but you've also got to be able to do the main thing: to know what to do with the bloody ball! At its simplest level that's what's wrong with British football today … too many people who can run all day but can't kick a ball!'

That was forty years ago but it rings true today. The emphasis on defensive football, team strategies and stamina in Britain has certainly denied opportunities to gifted individuals. Glen Hoddle of Spurs and England fame was beautifully balanced, with great vision, creative passing, and an excellent free-kick taker. In fact, he was one of the few British players in the 1980s to command the respect of foreign media and managers alike. Yet, Hoddle could never get a permanent place in the English team. When he was included he had to change his natural style so much that he looked constantly uncomfortable, and therefore under-confident. In most European or South American countries he'd have been made captain, hailed as a genius and retired as a national hero selling razor blades and health insurance.

The Golden Age of Brazil: attacking fullbacks

In the 1860s the English played football with one fullback.
In 1872 the Scots increased it to two.
In 1925 Herbert Chapman and Arsenal upped it to three.
In 1950 the Hungarians made it three and a half.
In 1958 the Brazilians made it four.

In the 1950 World Cup final, Uruguay used four defenders in a 'Swiss bolt' approach, and beat Brazil. The Brazilians, after recovering from the shock of defeat, decided 'never again'. They came up with a 4–2–4 pattern. As we have already seen, coaches and players had been experimenting with this idea, but it usually involved having a midfielder drop back to defend, as in the Hungarian system and the Swiss bolt. The Brazilians did it differently — they had an extra fullback (sometimes two) who could be used in both attack and defence. *Carumba*!

To make it work you needed really fit fullbacks with dribbling and passing skills and the ability to shoot. The attack-minded Brazil had these, and could throw as many as eight players forward at one time.

If this system had any weakness, it was in defence. Three players in the midfield is dangerously few, especially when everyone else was putting a new focus on defence and close marking in football.

Hungary reached the 1954 World Cup final using its version of 4–2–4, and only a tremendous injury toll from earlier games prevented it from winning. In 1958, in Sweden, Brazil won the

World Cup final using its more refined and flexible 4–2–4 system, which could quickly adapt into a 3–3–4 in attack, or 4–3–3 in defence. A new seventeen-year-old forward known as Pelé had a bit to do with the team's success as well. After the shock results in 1950 when Uruguay beat Brazil using the Swiss bolt, and again in 1954 when a dour West Germany beat up and then beat a badly injured Hungary, it was reassuring to know that the best team had won the World Cup.

Following the 1958 tournament, coaches and administrators in world football began to rethink their tactical approach. Television had something to do with it; suddenly footballers were in the limelight and if your team lost too many games, you could lose your job. Coaches realised that they could not 'out-attack' the Brazilians, especially with superstar players like Pelé in the team, and so not losing (and in particular not getting thrashed) became the focus, rather than winning. Victory became something you thought about after you'd made sure you'd escaped defeat.

The 1962 World Cup was the first example *en masse* of this new philosophy. Even Brazil showed up using a 4–3–3 system. Outrageously skilled individuals like Pelé, Puskas (Hungary) and Garrincha (Brazil) were now seen as assets only if they could be coached and disciplined into a defensive 4–3–3 strategy or the like. In the brave new world of defensive football, an undisciplined player was an unwanted player.

Goals are the proof of any system. At the World Cup in Switzerland in 1954, 26 games produced 140 goals at an average of 5.38 a game. Four years later in Sweden, despite an increase in the amount of matches to 35, total goals scored dropped to 126 at an average of 3.6, and by 1962 the average was down to a measly 2.78 per game. The low scores told the story: we had entered a dark and gloomy chapter in the story of world football.

The Dark Ages: the *catenaccio* takes hold

If the coming of the 4–3–3 system signalled the storm clouds gathering over the world's football horizon, then coaches in Italy were about to send the game into the Dark Ages. The Italians seized upon the Swiss bolt system, discarded after the 1950 World Cup finals and now completely forgotten by everyone except them, and by the early 1960s had perfected it, developing it into the *catenaccio* (literally, 'the chain'). By 1970, the word *catenaccio* was known and hated by football fans around the world as being synonymous with everything negative and destructive in modern football.

As with the 4–3–3 and the Swiss bolt itself, *catenaccio* was designed to *not lose* games rather than to win them. It began as 1–3–3–3, turned into 1–4–3–2, and at its peak (or rather depth) degenerated into 1–4–4–1. The key man was the *libero*, or sweeper, who patrolled the area behind the defensive backs, all of whom played tight man-to-man marking games, and sealed any gaps that remained. The idea was to strangle the opposition's offence, then rely on lightning-fast counter-attacks to score a goal. After scoring you went back into defensive mode and stayed there until the game ended. A score of 1–0 became a common result in Italian first division.

Catenaccio was certainly effective — it did make scoring extremely difficult for the other sides. But as a philosophy it was about as popular as a fart in a space suit. It just stank, big time. And it buried the talents of some of the most gifted players Italy has ever produced. In 1970 when Brazil, using a kind of 4–4–2 system, played Italy, who used a 'super-*catenaccio*' formation of 1–4–4–1, football had turned itself completely inside out. What had once been a joyous attacking game dominated by supremely skilled individuals had now become a boring corporate enterprise where individualists were seen as liabilities, and the fans, especially in Italy, had been largely forgotten. Could things get any worse? Most fans were afraid to ask.

Total football

In 1955, in an obscure little book called *Football Revolution*, former Austrian coach Willy Meisl wrote that football teams should look for all-rounders, players who can do anything and play any position:

> 'A fullback seeing an opening in front of him must seize his chance without hesitation. A wing half or winger will fall back, if necessary, and being an all-rounder will not feel out of place.'

In other words, defenders will attack, attackers will defend, and it will all happen at alarming speed. The *blitzkrieg* that could come from anywhere at any time. In fact, it came from Holland.

Up until 1970, the Dutch had enjoyed a long but unremarkable history in world football. Then, a Dutch club called Feyenoord won the European Cup. Far out. The next year another Dutch club, Ajax, won it again, then repeated their success in 1972, and in 1973 completed a hat-trick of European Cup victories. Something was definitely happening in Tulip Town. The 'something' was 'total football', and the man who made it happen was a player called Johan Cruyff. It arrived just in time to save the game from strangulation by defence-obsessed coaches.

The Dutch seemed to have borrowed the idea from the Swiss-bolt's inventor, Karl Rappan, 'that the team should outnumber its opposition in attack and defence' and combined it with the best aspects of Brazilian fluidity and rhythm in attack. The result was a kaleidoscope of movement, dazzling to watch and impossible to defend against.

Franz Beckenbauer, the German *libero supremo*, said in interview that the reason total football scared opposing teams and coaches to death was because they looked for the secret pattern and couldn't find it. In fact there was no pattern. Just like brilliant improvised jazz, everything was made up on the spot.

Total football was the last great tactical innovation in world football, and anyone who saw the Dutch national team with Cruyff as captain between 1970 and 1974 will never forget it. In the lead-up to the World Cup final in 1974, Holland won seven games, scoring fourteen goals and conceding just one. However, they fell at the final hurdle, just as Hungary had twenty years earlier, and were beaten 2–1 in the final by West Germany. Cruyff retired from international football after the 1974 finals, and total football, in its purest form, disappeared almost as magically as it had arrived just four years earlier.

In the 1990s we saw less and less of the old tactics and positions. Wingers disappeared and took centre-forwards with them. Teams like Argentina and Italy played with one forward at most, and he was almost certainly not the most creative player or main striker in the team. These could be found in the midfield along with almost everybody else.

Since total football, most developments in the game have been physical rather than tactical, and as defences have become bigger, fitter, faster and more cynical, the best players have faced a choice: either be systematically strangled, or keep away from the firing line. Maradona, Guillet Baggio, Platini and countless others have done just that. As a result, the midfield has become so overpopulated that sometimes it looks more like the white-goods department during the Boxing Day sale than a football field. It's not uncommon to see what is essentially a 4–5–1 system, or even the 3–6–1 formation that Senegal used to such great effect in Korea/Japan 2002.

The two most recent World Cup winners, France in 1998 and Brazil in 2002, have used formations based around midfield dominance, although both teams have also shown a greater than usual willingness to throw players forward. Of course, it helps if you have Zinedine Zidane or Ronaldinho pulling the strings in the middle of the park. The French of '98 played with an almost conventional 4–4–2, tweaked nicely with the four midfielders set up in a diamond formation for greater flexibility. Brazil played almost the whole team in midfield, arranged in a complicated 2–1–4–2–1 system that gave maximum options to move into attack or defence, with the supremely creative Ronaldinho and Rivaldo playing in the hole between true midfield and Ronaldo up front.

Brazil 2002

As this might suggest, the key to the modern game is flexibility — the capacity to respond to any changes in the game or imbalances in your team structure during a match. During Australia's last qualification game for the 2006 World Cup, against Uruguay in Sydney, coach Guus Hiddink's replacement of Tony Popovic with Harry Kewell changed the Socceroo's structure, and with it, the flow of the game — and ultimately, the result. Way to go, Guus!

Diving: a brief social history

There's not much that most football fans will agree on. Who was the best player ever, which was the greatest match, who scored the best goal — *no way ... he was offside by a mile!* Over such trivialities are marriages destroyed and lives torn apart. But there is one subject guaranteed to bring together bitter rivals and establish a brief truce: diving. Everybody hates it. It's cheating and is about as far removed as you can get from that elusive vision of sports administrators everywhere: the 'spirit of the game'. So where did it come from and how did it get here?

In the beginning was the game — a skill game based around dribbling. As the game evolved defenders tried to work out how to stop nimble–footed forwards or midfielders dancing around them like Fred Astaire. The response was simple, brutal, and effective. During the 1950s the cynical or 'professional' foul started to appear in the game; it involved a defender deliberately hacking or fouling the best attacking player on the opposition team.

At no time has this scenario been more real than in the lead up to the 1954 World Cup. The Hungarian national team led by 'the galloping major' Ferenc Puskas, a man whose stocky body belied his magical ability with the ball, was making the best defences in the world look like wooden soldiers. Coming into the finals, the Hungarians had been undefeated in four years and made their intentions clear in their opening game with a handy 9–0 win over South Korea. In their next game they came up against West Germany, whose defenders had a little surprise in store for Puskas and his boys. The Hungarians came out of the game victorious 8–3, but paid a heavy price. Puskas was kicked so badly and so often that he was unable to finish the game and played no further part in the tournament until the final, which he played despite still carrying injuries from this game. It should come as little surprise that West Germany emerged from the tournament as world champion — take that, spirit of the game!

By the mid-to-late sixties, the onset of football professionalism had made the professional foul commonplace. Elite players like Pelé, George Best, and Eusebio were being kicked out of the game. They were offered little in the way of protection from football officials and if they retaliated in frustration or self-defence they copped the brunt of the referee's displeasure. In Pelé's case, his treatment in the 1966 World Cup was so bad that he retired from international football.

In the 1970s, as defensive football became the norm, the whole emphasis of the game changed. Swashbuckling, 'balls to the wall', attacking football was almost extinct. The philosophy of the game had shifted from playing to win to a pragmatic emphasis on not losing at any cost. As defences became more packed and scoring opportunities became increasingly scarce, one method of scoring emerged that suited this new style of game: the set piece, or free kick. A team could pack ten men in defence and have a lone attacker halfway down the pitch. If he got the ball he was too isolated to be any real threat, but if he could run twenty-five metres into the opponent's half with the ball and win a free kick, then the cavalry could arrive to score a vital goal.

By the mid 1980s things had got so bad that the average first-division Italian match probably consisted of less than forty-five minutes actual playing time. The rest was taken up with endless free kicks from repetitive fouling, time-wasting by goalkeepers, and players taking throw-ins. It was a disgrace.

At the same time defensive tactics also became more subtle. Defenders realised that you didn't need to karate kick the opposition forwards off the park to prevent them from scoring when a well-timed nudge, elbow, tug of the shirt, or clip of the ankle would usually send an otherwise goal-bound shot into row eighty-seven in the grandstand. To response, forwards began exaggerating these sly fouls in order to bring the unseen to the referee's attention and so win another scoring opportunity. All understandable behaviour, but soon this kind of play-acting had evolved into the blight that we call diving. Forwards now very deliberately tried to win free kicks and penalties, even to the point of running at defenders instead of away from them, and slowing down to let them catch up, in order to 'draw a foul'. West Germany actually won the 1990 World Cup with a dive against Argentina.

An equally nauseating development in the modern game is referred to as 'simulation with intent' in FIFA newspeak. It translates as players making the most of an actual foul by writhing in exaggerated agony with the intention of not just winning a free kick, but getting their opponent yellow- or red-carded.

So, what's the solution? Use video replays wherever possible and hand out hefty suspensions if a player is found guilty of diving or simulation. It won't remove the problem completely, but it will make players and coaches think twice before selecting it as a tactical option. In the 1990s, FIFA began making changes to limit overly defensive play (red cards for professional fouls and no back-passing to the goalkeeper) in an attempt to bring back 'the beautiful game'. The same sort of action is now needed to relegate the actors back to the theatre and diving to the pool.

THE GREATEST SHOW ON EARTH

Uruguay 1930

Ladies and gentlemen, welcome to the greatest show on earth ... it's where?

The World Cup of football was the brain-child of FIFA's third president, Frenchman Jules Rimet. Although there had been earlier attempts to stage international football tournaments, they had withered on the vine and for a time FIFA had agreed to recognise the Olympic tournament as a de-facto world football championship. When the organising committee revealed that the 1932 Olympic Games would not include football, it was clear that FIFA would have to take the initiative and Rimet set about planning FIFA's own regular world championship.

But the World Cup was intended as more than just a sporting competition. Rimet was an idealist whose vision of the tournament had grown alongside the internationalist movement for peace that swept Europe in the aftermath of World War One. In this sense, the World Cup is a contemporary of the League of Nations, the precursor to the United Nations. Rimet had enormous optimism in the potential of football as a unifying force and believed that a truly international tournament which brought together nations in a spirit of friendly competition would help to diminish the threat of another Great War.

The first World Cup tournament was held in Uruguay in 1930. Uruguay had won the right to host the inaugural World Cup over Italy, Holland, Hungary, Spain, and Sweden. In typical European fashion, once their bids had failed the European nations had a collective attack of sour-grapes and withdrew from the tournament. In response, the Uruguayans offered to pay all their travel expenses (it was a three month round trip by sea in those days) but to no avail. To make matters worse, the British nations had withdrawn from FIFA in 1928 for a variety of reasons (some of them actually good) which left the Americas alone to compete for the title of world champion between themselves. Right at the death, Jules Rimet personally intervened and persuaded four European nations to attend the tournament and prevent it from becoming a farce.

Finally, the first World Cup got underway featuring thirteen countries, with the preliminary matches organised into four groups:

Group One
France, Mexico,
Argentina, Chile

Group Two
Yugoslavia, Brazil,
Bolivia

Group Three
Romania, Peru,
Uruguay

Group Four
USA, Belgium,
Paraguay

The winner of each group progressed to the semi-finals, where Argentina defeated the USA 6–1, and Uruguay defeated Yugoslavia with the same scoreline. This meant that the World Cup final would be a replay of the 1928 Olympic final where Uruguay had defeated its arch-rival, Argentina, 2–1 in a replay.

On July 30, 1930, the climax of a tournament that had included death threats to players and their families, crowd violence, allegations of match fixing and cheating by certain match officials, an all-in-brawl, and the intervention of the riot-squad, got underway in front of a crowd of ninety-three thousand in Montevideo's Centenario Stadium. Both teams used a 2–3–5 formation; that is, two defenders, three midfielders, and five forwards. While the rivalry between the players was understandably intense, relations between the two sets of fans and their respective governments were perhaps best described as hysterical. By the time the whistle blew at 2.30 p.m. to begin the final, both sides had declared war on each other but luckily they had confined the field of battle to the football pitch itself. When the dust settled a little over ninety minutes later, Uruguay had emerged victorious by a 4–2 scoreline and so the first world champions were crowned.

As a postscript to the tournament, Argentine officials broke off all relations with the Uruguayan Football Association citing threats and intimidation of their players. They also claimed that Uruguayan fans had deliberately kept the Argentine team awake the night before the big match by partying noisily outside their hotel — ring any bells, Socceroos? So much for the gentle ideals of fair play and good sportsmanship in the bygone days of the beautiful game.

Italy 1934

Il Duce ... Vittorio Pozzo and the rise of the Azzurri

The great achievement of the 1930 World Cup was the fact that it happened at all. Surely, if it could be done once then it could be done again. Having been turned down by FIFA as host for the 1930 tournament, the Italians wasted no time in renewing their efforts and in 1932 they were rewarded when it was announced that they had clinched the right to hold the second World Cup. This was particularly attractive to the Italians as Mussolini had been in power for ten years, and there is nothing a good fascist likes better than an international sporting event with its unique blend of nationalism, pomp, and ceremony. In the lead up to the tournament massive stadiums were built and Italian children were given pieces of brightly coloured ribbon to wave and lessons to fine-tune their fascist salutes for *Il Duce*.

Uruguay pulled out of the 1934 tournament, partly as pay-back for the Italian snub four years earlier and partly because of the very real possibility that they would not be able to successfully defend their title. England, Northern Ireland, Scotland, and Wales were still ineligible to compete due to their resignation from FIFA. Despite this, there was no shortage of applicants and eventually thirty-two teams nominated, forcing the organizers to stage a series of play-offs in order to reduce the number to the required sixteen. The finalists for the 1934 World Cup were: Italy, USA,

Czechoslovakia, Romania, Germany, Hungary, Belgium, Austria, France, Switzerland, the Netherlands, Sweden, Argentina, Egypt, Brazil, and Spain.

Going into the tournament the pick of the teams was undoubtedly the Austrians (the *Wunderteam*) who had put together a streak of eighteen games unbeaten. Close behind them were Vittorio Pozzo's Italy, Brazil, and Argentina. The tournament was organized on a strictly knockout basis which was particularly annoying to both Brazil and Argentina who, having travelled for three weeks just to get to Italy, went home after a first round defeat. The quarter-finals saw Sweden lose to Germany 1–2, Hugo Meisl's Austria defeat Hungary 2–1, Italy defeat Spain 1–0 via a replay after drawing 1–1, and Czechoslovakia overcome Switzerland 3–2.

Having overcome the Spanish and their legendary goalkeeper Zamorra, the hosts Italy now faced the Austrians, regarded by many as one of the great teams of all time. The Italian side was based around three key players — two of whom were in fact from Argentina. Luis Monti, the lynch-pin of the defence, had played for Argentina in the 1930 World Cup final and Raymondo Orsi, one of the finest wingers of the era, was also Argentine. However the marquee player for the *Azzurri* was Giuseppe Meazza, the centre-forward from Inter Milan who would later go on to captain the Italian national team and who became their greatest individual goal scorer until his record was finally broken in the 1970s. The Austrians were weakened by both age and injury. Added to this, the pitch was a quagmire that negated the beautiful passing game which had been the source of their many victories. A lone goal in the nineteenth minute by Enrico Guaita (also from Argentina) sealed a memorable 1–0 victory to put Italy through to the final where they would meet the surprise packet of the tournament: Czechoslovakia.

The final was held in Rome, under the hawk-like gaze of Mussolini who, up until then, had not shown the slightest interest in football. The *Azzurri* were strong favourites, but the Czechs were playing stylish football in the manner of the Austrians, and the Italians soon fell behind under sustained Czech pressure that resulted in a goal, midway through the second half. They say that you need a little luck to win a World Cup and the Italians got theirs via a Raymondo Orsi equalizer in the 82nd minute. As the game went into extra time the Italians looked the fitter and better side and when Schiavio put a tired shot past the Czech goalkeeper and captain Planicka, the title had been won by the host nation — again. An Italian journalist at the time observed that the opposition seems to do all the attacking but Italy wins the game — now why does that sound so familiar?

France 1938

The Black Diamond and his *bicicleta ... Forza Italia*

In 1938, as Europe was about to be plunged into chaos and war, the World Cup tournament was held in France, the home of its founder, Jules Reinet. A total of thirty-six teams entered, requiring another series of preliminary matches. British national teams were again absent due to their refusal to join FIFA, and the Spanish did not send a team due to the brutal civil war that was raging in Spain. But perhaps the team whose absence was most indicative of the period was Austria who, after qualifying through the play-offs as one of the final sixteen teams, was forced to withdraw on the eve of the tournament due to the fact that they had ceased to exist as a nation. When German troops marched over the border in March 1938 Austria became part of Nazi Germany, which meant that it could no longer compete independently. Several of Austria's finer players participated as part of the German team; but this didn't help the Germans much, as they were promptly eliminated by Switzerland, 4–2, in a replay, after drawing their first match. Italy scraped through against Norway, 2–1, and Brazil, featuring Leonidas, 'the Black Diamond', began their campaign with a 6–5 win over Poland.

The next round saw the Brazilians eventually defeat Czechoslovakia in a replay; their first encounter had degenerated into a punch-up in which three players were sent off, and then ended in a draw. In other matches, Sweden, who had gone straight through to the second round courtesy of the late Austrian withdrawal, finally entered the competition and promptly spanked Cuba 8–0, and the defending champions, Italy, defeated their French hosts 2–1. The semi-final pitted Italy against Brazil. So confident were the Brazilians that they rested key players, including top-scorer Leonidas, and booked all the seats on a flight to get to the final in Paris. But the Italians spoiled the party and triumphed, 2–1, and Brazil were on their way home. Hungary, who had beaten the Dutch East Indies and Switzerland on their way to the semis, crushed Sweden 5–1 and so earned the right to face the reigning world champions in the final.

The Italians played beautifully, defeating Hungary 4–2, with two goals each to Colaussi and the player of the tournament, Piola, and so retained their crowns as kings of world football to wear along with their gold medals from victory in the Berlin Olympic Games of 1936. Unfortunately, the *Azzurri* were denied the opportunity of a third successive victory, as the next World Cup would not be held for twelve years due to a rather rude and sustained interruption called World War II.

Brazil 1950

The little tournament that could ... the strange case of the Swiss bolt ... England comes in from the cold

As the twentieth century reached its halfway point, the nations of the world emerged from a period where the utter carnage of two world wars had been relieved only by the prolonged suffering of the Great Depression. On top of this loomed the impending nuclear rivalry of the Cold War and, to cap it all off, it had been twelve years since the last World Cup. The future of the tournament looked rocky, and football itself even seemed a bit trivial in light of the events of the previous decade. The turmoil of postwar Europe forced FIFA to look to South America to stage the championship, and so the right to host the fourth World Cup went to the only candidate who applied — Brazil.

The politics of international football has always been at least as complicated as conventional global diplomacy, and no sooner had FIFA formally declared Brazil host nation of the 1950 World Cup than the Soviet Union withdrew, Germany and Japan were suspended, and Austria, Scotland, and Turkey all qualified for the final tournament and then withdrew. Belgium, Finland, Peru, Ecuador, Burma, the Philippines, Indonesia, and Argentina filled out the cosmopolitan list of withdrawals, while Portugal and France waited until the last moment to decline their invitations to come and compete. India, after winning their qualifying group playing barefoot, refused to go to Brazil after FIFA ruled that their players would have to wear football boots if they wanted to participate in the finals. This left only thirteen teams to play for the World Cup instead of the required sixteen; but after the long break since France 1938 the organisers were determined to stage some sort of tournament and so get the ball rolling again.

Despite all the withdrawals, there was one new inclusion in Brazil that almost made up for the absentees — England, boasting Stanley Matthews and Tom Finney, made their World Cup debut after 20 years of self-imposed exile. The shortage of teams meant that round one of the 1950 World Cup tournament was made up of uneven groups:

Group One
Brazil, Mexico, Switzerland, Yugoslavia

Group Two
Spain, Chile, England, USA

Group Three
Sweden, Italy, Paraguay

Group Four
Uruguay, Bolivia

To compensate, there would be no semi-finals or finals; instead, each group winner would progress to a group of four finalists who would each play one another, with the eventual winner of the group being crowned World Champions.

Brazil won Group One, with two victories and a surprising, two-all draw against the Swiss, who utilised a formation known as the *verrou*, or 'Swiss bolt' to contain the home side and achieve this remarkable result (see section on tactics). Spain aced Group Two with three wins, but the real story of the group was England, who lost 1–0 to Spain and (unbelievably) 1–0 to the USA — many pundits still regard this as the greatest upset in football history. Group three was tight, with Sweden edging out Italy on goal difference; and in the sole game in Group Four, Uruguay squeaked home 8–0 against Bolivia.

And so the final group games began: unconvincing qualifiers Uruguay held utterly convincing Spain to a two-all draw. Brazil began in typically uncertain fashion with a 7–1 annihilation of Sweden. Uruguay got the shell-shocked Swedes next, and dispatched them 3–2 in a cliff-hanger. Brazil scraped by with another lucky 6–1 victory over Spain, thereby setting up a final, of sorts, against Uruguay.

The venue was the Maracana Stadium with a capacity of two hundred thousand spectators. Brazil, who boasted Ademir, Zizinho, and Jair, were unbackable favourites. Uruguay hadn't even qualified, but were invited to compete and given the soft group against only Bolivia by prior arrangement. Even their own official delegation gave them no chance, one remarking that a 4–0 loss would be a victory of sorts. But Uruguay was not a team of no-hopers; rather they were a team in the middle of a rebuilding phase. In defence they had Obdulio Varela and Victor Andrade; in goal, Rogue Maspoli; and in attack, Alcide Ghiggia and Juan Schiaffino.

The first half was all Brazil, but the onslaught also had the effect of galvanising the experienced Uruguayan defence. Somehow, they held out until half-time preserving a scoreline of nil-all, but the spirit inside the Maracana was still a joyous carnivale: surely it was just a matter of time before Brazil registered their dominance on the scoreboard. Sure enough, in the second half the Brazilians scored virtually from the kick-off to finally take the lead 1–0, but the balance of play suggested that it should have been 5–0 and that this would come back to haunt the Brazilians.

Uruguay had used a version of the Swiss bolt to keep themselves in the game; now, seeking an equaliser, they began to turn it into attack. Despite the fact that Brazil only needed a draw to win the tournament, they could not curb their attacking instinct to concentrate on defence. Midway through the second half, Schiaffino headed home a cross from Ghiggia to level the scores at 1–1. Suddenly the massive crowd went quiet as the unthinkable began to dawn on 200,000 fans — Brazil might lose! Sensing a historic opportunity, Uruguay went on all-out attack. In the seventy-ninth minute Ghiggia, who was creating havoc, met a pass wide on the right and, as the defence looked for him to again cross to Schiaffino in the centre, he drilled home the winner at the near post.

Uruguay hung on for the final ten minutes to achieve the unlikeliest victory in a World Cup final thus far. It came as such a shock that when the 1950 World Cup trophy was presented to Uruguay, officials forgot to play their national anthem, and when the players took their traditional lap of honour the stadium was virtually empty. Such was the magnitude of Brazil's failure to win the trophy at home that people wept openly in the streets and several suicides were reported. After four tournaments, the World Cup scoreboard stood at Italy 2, Uruguay 2, and good luck to everyone else.

Switzerland 1954

Happy FIFA fiftieth ... the battle of Berne ... Hungarian rhapsody in blue

The finals of the fifth World Cup tournament were held in Switzerland to celebrate fifty years since FIFA had been founded in Zurich by Jules Rimet. Going into the fifth tournament a number of truisms had emerged, some of which still resonate with fans of the world game:

1. Brazil were always favourites (or at least equal favourites) to win — this was despite never having won the tournament and having lost twice after being unbackable favourites.
2. South Americans struggle to win in Europe and the Europeans return the favour in South America.
3. Italy always produces over cautious, counter-attacking players (let's face it, it's genetic).
4. England were never as good as they think they were.
5. The final was rarely contested by the two best teams in the tournament.

The fifth World Cup was notable for many reasons, but three stand out in particular: both television and Asia (in the form of Korea) made their debuts in Switzerland, and the tournament averaged nearly five-and-a-half goals per game — an amazingly high figure. The 1954 tournament also featured probably the greatest team never to win the World Cup, although the Dutch might argue that point. I speak of Hungary, the mighty Magyars, who included the great Ferenc Puskas, Sandor Kocsis, Nandor Hidgekuti, and Joszef Bozsik, to name but a few. Rated as second favourite was (you guessed it) Brazil. Also mentioned in dispatches were Italy and Uruguay, but the talk of the tournament was to be all about the Hungarians. Coming into the 1954 World Cup they were on a four-year, twenty-eight game unbeaten run that included demolitions of England, 6–3 at Wembley, and again 7–1 in Budapest, and Italy 3–0 in Italy

Again, the tournament began with sixteen teams organised in four groups, and again a new system for the preliminary games was tried. This time, two seeded teams were placed in each group who would not play each other, whatever happened. The groups were:

Group One
Brazil, Mexico,
France, Yugoslavia

Group Two
Hungary, Turkey,
Korea, West Germany

Group Three
Uruguay, Scotland,
Austria, Czechoslovakia

Group Four
England, Belgium,
Italy, Switzerland

From Group One, Brazil and Yugoslavia qualified for the second round, while Hungary and West Germany went through from Group Two — West Germany requiring a play-off to defeat Turkey. In Group Three, Uruguay and Austria smashed their opponents to book their places in the quarter-finals; and in the final group, England and Switzerland went through to the second round, but only after the Swiss had survived a play-off against Italy.

The quarter-finals provided some intriguing match-ups on paper: West Germany vs Yugoslavia, Austria vs Switzerland, Uruguay vs England, and Hungary vs Brazil — and reality did not disappoint. The Germans defeated Yugoslavia 2–0 by butchering them so badly that they played the majority of the match with nine men — there were no sissy-boy substitutions in those days, bucko! In complete contrast, Switzerland set a record by scoring five goals in their quarter-final and still being eliminated by Austria, who managed a lazy seven in reply. Uruguay carved up England 4–2 with little trouble, and the quarter-finals were rounded out by a match that pitted the two top teams, Hungary and Brazil, against each other.

The match is remembered as 'the Battle of Berne'. It featured three players being sent off, two penalties, and an all-in-brawl after the final whistle that spilled into the dressing rooms and the car park, and involved players, officials, and spectators. Oh, and by the way, Hungary won 4–2. To set the record straight, the match also revealed a facet of the Brazilian game that is often over-looked. While they are famous for playing *jogo bonito* ('the beautiful game') and are a joy to watch, they can also be real mon-grels when they want to and can punch, kick, spit, and dive with the worst of them.

The semi-final between Hungary and Uruguay is remembered as one of the greatest games ever played. It was end-to-end stuff, and two goals to Uruguay's Hohberg and one each to Czibor and Hidegkuti saw the scores locked at 2–2 at full-time. In extra time the great Sandor Kocsis scored twice in five minutes to help Hungary inflict Uruguay's first-ever loss in a World Cup match. In the other semi-final, West Germany smashed Austria 6–1, and so the final of the 1954 World Cup was to be played between Hungary and West Germany. As is often the case, the final would not be played between the two best teams in the tournament. And if this was an example of typically cruel football justice, then, cru-eler still, the final result was to prove that the best team does not always win the World Cup.

Hungary started favourites, but they were severely weakened by injury and fatigue. Their great forward Ferenc Puskas had not been able to play since the first round, when the West German defence, led by Werner Liebrich, had kicked the shit out of him. The team was also drained after two epic encounters against Brazil and Uruguay. Despite not being fully fit, Puskas insisted on taking the field, and seemed to have vindicated his judgment when he scored after only six minutes. Two minutes later Hungary scored again through Czibor to stretch their lead to 2–0. But, sadly for the Hungarians, Puskas was to have little influence on the rest of the game; he was virtually a passenger from then on. On top of this, the weather seemed to turn against them. The match had been played in gentle rain, which all of a sudden became a deluge that turned the pitch into a mud-bath, enabling the Germans to claw their way back and level the score at 2–2.

With only seven minutes to go, West Germany took a 3–2 lead when winger Helmut Rahn scored his second goal for the match. Puskas replied immediately for Hungary to again level the scores, but his goal was disallowed for offside. 'We wuz robbed', cried Hungary — and they were probably right. But it didn't make any difference to the final result, as West Germany won the first of their three trophies in a result that Germans still refer to as the miracle of Berne.

Sweden 1958

Swedish modern ... the new king is crowned ... the new empire begins

The sixth World Cup, held in Sweden, heralded the debut of arguably the game's greatest and certainly its single most influential player: Edson Arantes do Nascimento, aka Pele ... but more of him later. In the four years since their unlikely victory in the 1954 final, West Germany, the defending champion, had basically done nothing. Their opponents in the final, Hungary, were also a shadow of the once-mighty Magyars. Following the 1956 Soviet invasion, Puskas, Czibor, and Kocsis — all irreplaceable members of the national team — had refused to return home and were therefore not considered for selection.

The final groupings looked like this:

Group One
West Germany, Northern Ireland, Argentina, Czechoslovakia

Group Two
France, Yugoslavia, Scotland, Paraguay

Group Three
Sweden, Mexico, Hungary, Wales

Group Four
England, Brazil, Austria, USSR

At a glance, Group Four was definitely the first bona fide 'group of death'. England had suffered from its self-imposed exile from FIFA but still provided strong competition. The Soviet Union were another team to have come in from the cold, and could boast among its number Lev Yashin, regarded by many as the finest goalkeeper to have played the game. Brazil were ... Brazil, but with the added ingredient of the seventeen-year-old Pele. Last but not least was Austria, a stalwart of the World Cup and a country with a rich football history and culture.

And so the games began. From Group One, West Germany and (after a play-off) tiny Northern Ireland progressed to the quarter-finals at the expense of Argentina, whose squad had been ravaged by defections to Italian clubs (most notably Omar Sivori). In another upset, the depleted Hungarians found themselves eliminated from Group Three as Sweden and Wales marched on into the next round. Unsurprisingly, France and Yugoslavia went through from Group Two to join them.

The 'group of death' lived up to its name. Brazil, which, alongside the young Pele, featured players such as Vava, Didi, Garrincha, and Nilton Santos, aced the group, but not without the scare of a 0–0 draw with England. With two other draws from their group matches, the English forced a play-off with the USSR, which the Soviets won 1–0 to join the Brazilians in the second round.

The quarter-finals saw France thump a brave Northern Ireland 4–0, West Germany defeat Yugoslavia 1–0, and Sweden dispatch the Soviet Union 2–0. In the final match of the second round, Brazil struggled to overcome Wales by a single goal (Pele's first World Cup goal). Would they fail again? The semi-final pitted them against France, who had progressed thus far thanks mainly to the extraordinary goal-scoring feats of Just Fontaine. Fontaine maintained his solid average (he was to finish the tournament with a tally of 13 goals — a record), scoring early in the semi-final, but he was eclipsed by a superb hat-trick to Pele. With one goal each to Vava and Didi, Brazil won comfortably 5–2. In the other semi-final the Swedes came from behind to defeat West Germany, who played the final half-hour with only ten men, 3–1.

So Brazil would meet the hosts, Sweden, in the final. Things looked good for the home team early, and Liedholm capped off a brilliant piece of team play to give the Swedes a 1–0 lead after only four minutes. The Brazilians were widely seen as front-runners, and many of the fifty thousand crowd believed that being a goal behind would disrupt their free-flowing style of play. But this thought was dispelled almost immediately when Vava scored from a superb Garrincha cross to level 1–1. On the half-hour mark he scored a second to give the Brazilians a 2–1 lead at half-time. The second half belonged to Brazil and to the mercurial teenager Pele in particular: he scored twice and created another as Brazil ran out winners 5–2, securing the trophy for the first time and establishing the most successful reign in football history.

Chile 1962

The battle of Santiago ... the Black Cat and the Little Bird ... 'Pele was the best but Garrincha was better'

CAMPEONATO MUNDIAL DE FUTBOL
WORLD FOOTBALL CHAMPIONSHIP
CHAMPIONNAT MONDIAL DE FOOTBALL
COUPE JULES RIMET

CHILE
1962

World Cup number seven was held in Chile, to virtually everyone's surprise including most Chileans. Since its resurrection in 1950, the tournament had grown steadily at every level due to the increasing membership of FIFA, and especially thanks to the growing coverage on television, which took it to an audience of millions around the world. The tournaments themselves had developed into brilliant, dramatic spectacles with a star to headline each World Cup. In 1950 and 1958 Brazil had burned bright, and in 1954 the magnificent Hungarians had been the marquee names. Unfortunately, every World Cup cannot be a classic. Every stone is not a diamond, and all that glitters is not gold. My grandma used to say that 'even Jesus had a day off' — which brings us nicely to the 1962 tournament.

Forgettable is probably too-high praise for World Cup number seven. Forty-nine nations entered, with only sixteen qualifying for the final tournament in Chile — ultimately, most of those that missed out were pleased that they had. The sixteen qualifiers for the 1962 World Cup were:

Group One
Yugoslavia, Uruguay,
Colombia, USSR

Group Two
Chile, West Germany
Switzerland, Italy

Group Three
Brazil, Mexico,
Spain, Czechoslovakia.

Group Four
England, Hungary,
Argentina, Bulgaria

The first round was more notable for who was sent home rather than who went through. Uruguay, Italy, Spain, and Argentina all fell at the first hurdle. The round's one outstanding feature was 'the battle of Santiago', in which a brilliant Italian team took on the hosts, Chile. Unfortunately for the *Azzurri*, an Italian journalist who had been dispatched to cover the tournament had spent his time in Chile filing stories about what a miserable, third world country it was. The choicest extracts from these had been reprinted in the Chilean press and had successfully enraged the people. When the Italian team took the field it was like walking into a hornet's nest. Two Italians were sent off, and players were punched and kicked behind play, during play, in front of play, and (like Berne in 1954) in the dressing-room after play. The English referee admitted that he had wanted to abandon the game at half-time but was afraid of what might happen if he did. Chile ran out eventual winners, 2–0, and the Italians were probably happy to be on their way home.

The quarter-finals produced the following match-ups: Yugoslavia vs. West Germany, Brazil vs. England, Chile vs. USSR, and Czechoslovakia vs. Hungary. Yugoslavia finally got revenge for twice being eliminated by the Germans when they defeated West Germany 1–0; Brazil (despite missing the injured Pele) accounted for England 3–1; the Czechs outplayed the Hungarians for a 1–0 result; and Chile upset the USSR 2–1. The hosts had probably exceeded all expectations by making it as far as the semi-final, but their luck ran out when they encountered a rampant Brazil who politely dissected them 4–2, courtesy of two goals each to Vava and the star of the tournament, Garrincha. In the other semi, the Czechs and Yugoslavia seemed evenly matched and went in at half-time at 0–0; but in the second half Czechoslovakia kicked away to a 3–1 victory, thanks mainly to a double to Scherer.

Going into the final, the big talking point was whether Garrincha, who had been sent off in the semi-final against Chile, would be allowed to take his place in the final against Czechoslovakia. Ultimately, 'the little bird' was allowed to play, and he inspired his team to a 3–1 win to record back-to-back World Cup victories. Brazil, Italy, and Uruguay now each claimed two titles a piece as the world waited for FIFA to announce the European hosts of the 1966 World Cup.

England 1966

A dog called pickles and the case of the vanishing trophy ... The Black Pearl ... Rule Brittania: the most controversial goal of all

For the eighth World Cup finals, FIFA decided to return to the birthplace of modern football — England. The original rules of the game had been drawn up there in 1863 and the first international ever staged was played between England and Scotland in 1872, so in terms of football pedigree there could be no question of England's worthiness as hosts. However, in the mid-1960s it wasn't just football that was driving England to the centre of the world stage. A revolution in music, cinema, and fashion was sweeping the globe, and the British beat was the hottest cultural item on the planet. Bands like The Beatles, The Rolling Stones, The Who, The Yardbirds, and The Animals were creating the soundtrack to a social, cultural, and political revolution that was without precedent. Aided by the growth of television, radio, and cinema, the 'green and pleasant land' had become the absolute epicentre of everything that was hip and cool in youth culture.

English football clubs had also been making inroads into European club competition, with Tottenham (in 1963) and West Ham (in 1965) having won the European Cup Winner's Cup. Other forces were also at work, stimulating the growth of the tournament itself until it had become as unstoppable as Topsy. Professionalism was now the norm for players in most European countries, thanks mainly to the incredible popularity of football as a television sport. Driven by sponsorship and advertising money, TV was also transforming football players into genuine stars with powerful mass appeal and influence. Basically, the cliché of going from strength to strength was never more apt than in describing the state of football in 1966.

The sixteen finalists were:

Group One
England, Mexico,
France, Uruguay

Group Two
West Germany, Argentina,
Spain, Switzerland

Group Three
Brazil, Bulgaria,
Hungary, Portugal

Group Four
Italy, North Korea
Chile, USSR

With the coming of full-time professionalism to some countries but not others, the performance gap was growing wider. The teams expected to do well in England were: Brazil (as always), USSR, Portugal, Italy, West Germany, and England. Others rated a fair chance included Argentina, Hungary, and France.

After their rude introduction to World Cup football in 1950, the English had begun the slow process of learning and rebuilding to make up for their long years of self-imposed exile from FIFA. In the 1960s, this was starting to pay dividends; their coach, Alf Ramsey, had the nucleus of a side that, on paper, looked very difficult to beat. In goal was Gordon Banks, thought by some to be better than Yashin; Bobby Moore, an immensely talented and statesman-like leader, was centre-back; Martin Peters, his West Ham team-mate, was an extremely capable mid-fielder; and, in Bobby Charlton and Jimmy Greaves, England had two of the most highly rated goal scorers in the game.

Portugal was based almost entirely on the magnificent Benfica team — one of the leading clubs in Europe at the time. With Torres at the back, Mario Coluna in mid-field, and the explosive Eusebio up front, they could hurt you from anywhere. Brazil still had great names like Garrincha, Pele, and Djalma Santos, but in truth were a side in decline. Under the tutelage of coach Vincent Feola, they were in a period of rebuilding from the glory days of 1958 and 1962.

West Germany looked very strong. Coach Sepp Herberger, who had been at the helm since Columbus discovered the New World, had finally retired. His replacement, Helmut Schon, would quickly become a legend in European and World football. On the field, Uwe Seeler had matured into a brutally efficient centre-forward, while Franz 'the Kaiser' Beckenbauer and Wolfgang Overath came together to form one of the finest midfield combinations on the planet.

The Italians, like the Germans, also had a new coach and a strong side. Edmondo Fabbri had taken his club Mantova from division four to division one in just seven years as coach. Giacinto Facchetti of Inter Milan was the lynch-pin of the Italian defence. Extremely tall and deceptively quick, he was an attacking full-back without peer. In front of him were Sandro Mazzola and Giani Rivera, two of the most technically gifted players Italy has ever produced.

The first round of the tournament got under way with a blend of shocking upsets and business as usual. In Group One, England and Uruguay progressed through to the quarter-finals, but neither team looked impressive. Uruguay used a very negative defensive strategy that relied on counter-attacking to score goals. And indeed this seemed to be the pattern that was indicative of a new philosophy taking over the world game. Playing for a draw, playing not to lose or, in some cases, just kicking the shit out of talented opponents to the point that they couldn't play, had for many teams replaced the whole notion of playing to win as the primary focus of the game. In Group Two, West Germany and Argentina went through to the next round with game plans based on well-organised defence but with a sting in front of goal.

Group three provided the two big shocks of the tournament: one was the elimination of Brazil; the second was the way they were eliminated. First, Brazil managed to beat Bulgaria 2–0 in the opening game, but at a huge cost. Pele was kicked off the park and given no protection by the match officials, and several other Brazilians were also injured during the match. Next, they met Hungary, led by Florian Albert, who carved them up mercilessly 3–1. In their final match, a re-jigged but still undermanned Brazil met tournament hot-shots Portugal. Playing for their survival in the tournament, again they were butchered without mercy, but this time they also succumbed to the skill of tournament top-scorer Eusebio, who put away a neat double to send the Brazilians home. After the match, a battered Pele vowed to never again play in a World Cup. Hungary and Portugal went through to the second round.

Group four provided another surprise elimination — one that ranks as perhaps the second-biggest upset in World Cup history. The Soviet Union, playing a mechanistic brand of football, won all three matches and qualified first. The battle was on for second place. Italy won their opening game against Chile 2–0, but looked completely unconvincing. Next they lost 1–0 to the USSR, setting up a last-game, must-win clash against the tournament's minnows, North Korea. On paper, it looked like a gimme for the Italians; but then, as a lot of people have said, games aren't played on paper. North Korea's only real asset was speed, and lots of it; but, amazingly, Italy picked a slow and not fully fit team. The North Koreans proceeded to run the out-of-form Italians off their feet. When Giacomo Bulgarelli re-injured himself and came off after half an hour, the Italians were reduced to ten men, and it was only minutes later that the Koreans got the goal they thoroughly deserved and joined the Soviets in the next round.

The quarter-finals were thus: North Korea vs. Portugal, England vs. Argentina, USSR vs. Hungary, and West Germany vs. Uruguay.

In the first match against Portugal, the North Koreans came out and scored three unanswered goals in twenty minutes. Even they looked stunned. Then came a cruel but swift reality-check in the form of four Eusebio goals, plus a fifth to Augusto, and Portugal ran out 5–3 winners. The USSR basically bored their opponents to death with ponderous football that got them home 2–1 against the more artistic Hungarians. The other two quarter-finals were classic Europe vs. South America confrontations, and controversy continues to this day in the fall-out from these two matches. In the Uruguay vs. West Germany match, the English referee sent off two Uruguayans, and the Germans strolled home 4–0. In the other quarter-final, the German referee sent off Argentine captain Rattin, 'for the look in his eye' no less! England got home 1–0 with some difficulty.

The semi-finals saw England finally click and defeat Portugal 2–1, thanks mainly to Nobby Stiles' ability to push Eusebio out of the game, but also thanks to a double to Bobby Charlton. West Germany saw off the USSR 2–1, and so the final was decided: England would play its arch-rival, West Germany.

The final itself proved to be as dramatic and controversial as any ever staged. West Germany led after thirteen minutes via a Helmut Haller shot, but England equalised almost immediately through a Geoff Hurst header. For almost an hour the game see-sawed between the two teams, the tension becoming almost unbearable. With just over twelve minutes remaining, Martin Peters put England ahead, 2–1. Could they hang on to secure their first World Cup victory? In the last minute of normal time the

Germans were awarded a free kick, and Wolfgang Weber was able to put home the equaliser. At 2–2, the match went to extra time.

Eight minutes into extra time, Geoff Hurst scored the single most-debated goal in football history. On the end of a cross from Alan Ball, Hurst struck a thunderous shot against the cross-bar which bounced down and then out of the German goal. The referee didn't know what had happened, so he consulted the Soviet linesman: a goal! In 2003 a team of British physicists finally proved that it was definitely a goal ... but then, they were British. Anyway, Hurst scored again to claim a vital hat-trick and to put the English victory beyond doubt: 4–2. The match had been televised, either live or on replay, all around the globe. The modern era had arrived.

Mexico 1970

The greatest of them all? ... High noon at the Aztec Stadium starring Edson Arantes do Nascimento and his all dancing _jogo bonito_ revue

The ninth World Cup drew a record seventy-one entrants; so play-offs, beginning two years earlier, were staged to accommodate everyone and reduce the teams to the final sixteen. Mexico was chosen as host following its successful hosting of the 1968 Olympic Games. This was despite strenuous objections on medical grounds about the negative effects of extreme heat and altitude:

Australia's Ron Clarke had nearly died during the Olympics, and many other athletes in middle-distance and long-distance events had collapsed or withdrawn due to altitude sickness. The growing influence of television on the greatest show on earth was evident in FIFA's decision to hold several key matches, including the final, in the searing midday heat of Aztec Stadium to coincide with European prime-time TV slots. This decision was to have great ramifications on certain key matches during the tournament.

Nineteen seventy also saw the introduction of two very positive initiatives from FIFA: the yellow and red card system for foul play, and two substitutes per game.

The fancied teams were defending champions England, West Germany, Italy, and, you guessed it . . . Brazil. Peru was the favourite roughie, having eliminated Argentina in qualification. If anything, England looked a stronger squad than the one that had lifted the trophy four years earlier. To allow themselves to properly acclimatise, they had arrived in Mexico four weeks before the tournament kicked off, bringing with them their own chefs and food supply. Their opponents from the 1966 final, West Germany, also looked to be a stronger unit this time, especially with the inclusion of goal-scoring phenomenon Gerd 'der Bomber' Mueller from Bayern Munich up front. The Italians were playing under the spell of the *catanaccio*, and boasted a quite brilliant if overly cautious counter-attacking team that included Gianni Rivera, Sandro Mazzola, the goal-scoring left-back Giacinto Facchetti, and Gigi Riva ('rombo di tuono' — the clap of thunder). Such was the power of Riva's left foot that he once broke a child's arm with a free kick that had gone over the crossbar and into the crowd. However, all of these teams had one enormous disadvantage in common — they were Europeans, and this was Central America.

After the disappointment of 1966, Brazil had gone through quite a rebuilding process involving new coaches, new players, and new tactics. Coming into the tournament their squad included men such as Carlos Alberto, Jairzinho, Tostao, Gerson, Rivelino — and, of course, the king, Pele.

The preliminary groups looked like this:

Group One
Mexico, Belgium
El Salvador, USSR

Group Two
Italy, Uruguay,
Sweden, Israel

Group Three
England, Romania,
Brazil, Czechoslovakia

Group Four
West Germany, Peru,
Bulgaria, Morocco

If Group Three was not a genuine 'group of death', it was at the very least a 'group of critical injury'.

The hosts, Mexico, after following the tradition of a dull, goalless draw to begin proceedings, went on to notch up two victories and qualify along with the USSR from Group One. Group Two saw Italy and Uruguay go through. As if to emphasise their new-found passion for defensive football, the Italians scored one goal in three matches, despite having goal-scorers such as Riva, Rivera, and Mazzola. In Group Three, England and Brazil went through and produced the best match of the tournament thus far. In a wonderful display of elegant, tactical football, Brazil got home 1–0 over the English, who missed a virtually open goal late in the game which would have given them a well-deserved draw. In Group Four, West Germany and Peru proved too strong, the latter showing flashes of real brilliance in their two wins. So the quarter-finals were: Uruguay vs. USSR, Italy vs. Mexico, Brazil vs. Peru, and West Germany vs. England.

In the first quarter-final, Uruguay defeated the predictable Soviets 1–0. Italy, having reached the play-or-perish stage of the tournament, destroyed Mexico 4–1 in a display that caught everybody's attention. Plucky Peru were unlucky in having to play Brazil, who were irresistible in beating them 4–2. The last quarter-final was a replay of the controversial 1966 final between England and West Germany. Trailing by two goals, the Germans rallied and scored twice to level the score and send the game into extra time, during which Gerd Muller got the winner, and sweet revenge.

The semi-final match-ups ensured a European vs. South American final, when West Germany drew the suddenly in-form Italians, and Brazil were drawn to meet their old foes, Uruguay. The first semi-final produced a game that, for many commentators and fans, has gone down in history as the greatest football match ever played. As a spectacle, it transcended mere sport to become great human theatre full of tragedy, triumph, despair, ecstasy, and controversy ... the whole nine yards.

The Italians came out looking for an early goal and got one after only seven minutes through Boninsegna. Immediately, in true *catanaccio* style, they went into ultra-defence to close the game down. In the blazing midday sun of the Aztec Stadium, the Germans hammered and probed, and probed and hammered at the Italian defensive wall. Nothing. Beckenbauer launched another attacking raid and was brutally hacked down on the edge of the box, dislocating his shoulder. With no fresh substitutes available to come on, he simply had his arm strapped across his chest and played on. Of such stuff are legends made.

With one minute remaining, Karl-Heinz Schnellinger scored for West Germany to send the game into extra time. The Germans were euphoric; the Italians, exhausted and devastated. Five minutes into extra time the Germans scored again through Muller to lead 2–1; but their joy was short-lived as Burgnich replied almost immediately to again draw the Italians level. Minutes before the end of the first half of extra time, Gigi Riva finally got away from his marker to put Italy ahead 3–2; but not for long, as the irrepressible Muller equalised again for West Germany five minutes into the second half. It was surreal: the heat, the altitude, the exhaustion, the pressure of a World Cup semi-final. Fans, officials, and even some players stood and stared in a kind of uncomprehending stupor. But not Gianni Rivera, who received a pass, evaded his marker, and slotted the ball home to put Italy up 4–3. Before play could restart, the referee blew full-time. Players collapsed, too tired to celebrate or even to mourn. Finally, it was over, and the Italians had won a famous victory — but the toll that it took on them was to become all-too-clear in the final. In the other semi-final, Brazil struggled to overcome a determined Uruguay before eventually running out winners, 3–1.

The final would see perhaps the greatest attacking team in football history up against the masters of defence and counter-attack. Unsurprisingly, the Italians started cautiously, packing their defence with players like links in a chain. Finally, Pele headed home a cross from Rivelino to open the scoring for Brazil. But just before half-time, Boninsegna equalised for Italy. Brazil looked great in attack, but the Italians had shown in their two previous games that they could score goals (they had managed eight in the quarter and semi-finals) and that, mentally, they were never beaten. However, this time the dressing room at half-time told a different story — the Italians were gone, exhausted by the effort of their semi-final victory. There is no evidence to say that, had they been fresh, they could have changed the final result; but what is certain is that, as they ran out to take the field for the second half, only eleven substitutes could have given them a chance.

Brazil carved them up, with goals to Gerson, Jairzinho, and Carlos Alberto. Brazil 4, Italy 1, in a victory for the beautiful game, with positive football triumphing over cynicism. The 1970 world champions, Brazil, are still widely regarded as the greatest team of all time. As the dark cloud of negative 'professionalism' settled in, complete with time wasting, defensive play, professional fouls, and a brutal belief in victory after any fashion, one last magnificent sunset of brilliant colour had marked the passing of an era ... or had it?

FuBball-Weltmeisterschaft 1974
FIFA World Cup 1974
Coupe du Monde de la FIFA 1974
Copa Mundial de la FIFA 1974

West Germany 1974

**The clockwork orange ...
Beckenbauer bares all ...
'football begins afterwards'**

Football as a professional, international sport continued to develop at an extraordinary pace, and each World Cup tournament served as a showcase of the game's progress over the previous four years. The tenth World Cup finals, held in West Germany, made it clear for all to see that football was now big business, involving huge sums of money. The host's payoff from the 1974 tournament would be in excess of US$40 million, and player pay-disputes threatened the appearance of at least three of the sixteen finalists, including one of the pre-tournament favourites, Holland.

Politics continued to assert an unwelcome influence on the game, producing one of the strangest and certainly the most one-sided game in history. The Soviet Union had been drawn to play Chile in the pre-tournament qualification round. After a nil-all draw in Moscow the return match at the National Stadium in Santiago was thrown on its head when, in Chile, the elected Allende government was overthrown by a brutal right-wing military junta. The USSR refused to play the return leg in Santiago, pointing out (correctly) that the stadium had been used as a centre for the detention and torture of political prisoners. When their request for a neutral venue was denied by FIFA they withdrew, and the Chilean team took the field against no opposition. In a bizarre, football pantomime, the referee blew his whistle, and Chile kicked off and dribbled downfield to score, and post a 1–0 victory to qualify.

The other event of great note was the debut of Australia at the World Cup finals. If only we'd known that it would take thirty-two years to do it again we would have all gone over and taken our Bell & Howell home-movie cameras — hindsight is a marvellous thing. The sixteen finalists were:

Group One
West Germany, Chile,
Australia, East Germany

Group Two
Brazil, Scotland,
Yugoslavia, Zaire

Group Three
Netherlands, Bulgaria,
Sweden, Uruguay

Group Four
Italy, Argentina,
Poland, Haiti

Alongside Australia, Haiti and Zaire also made their debut in 1974, and the presence of this trio divided opinion as to the worthiness of their participation. One school of thought held that only the best sixteen teams in the world should be entitled to compete and that, if this was the case, there would be no teams from anywhere in Asia, Africa, or Oceania. With the increasing revenue being generated by the tournament, these voices were getting louder. On the other hand, there were many who loved the cosmopolitan nature of the World Cup: the fact that it was a celebration of the world game, and recognition that the world was bigger than just Europe and South America.

The 1974 tournament began without a clear-cut favourite. Brazil was rated a contender simply because they were Brazil, but they had lost most of the triumphant team of 1970. West Germany, the hosts, were worthy European champions and had great players like Beckenbauer, Muller, and Overath at the peak of their powers. For the first time since its re-entry into FIFA, England had failed to qualify. They had been beaten by an extraordinarily gifted Polish team that had also won the Olympic gold medal at Munich in 1972; the Poles again looked very capable, although they had little experience at this level.

And then there were the Dutchmen, led by the enigmatic genius Johan Cruyff. While the Dutch national team had never really lived up to its potential, 'the clockwork orange' (as they were christened thanks to the almost mechanical efficiency of their team play) were confirmed as the neutral's favourite, based almost entirely on the white-hot form of Dutch clubs Ajax and Feyenoord. The coming of professionalism to Holland had revolutionised Dutch football, sending them from zeroes to heroes overnight. On top of this was their almost mystical approach to the game — 'total football'. The Dutch style of game was the new order in world football and was proving to be as irresistible as it was unintelligible to other teams, as Dutch clubs dominated Europe's premier club competition, winning four European Cups in a row. Perennial slow-starters Italy would be there or thereabouts; and if they made it through to round two, only a fool would bet against them. And, of course, Argentina and the ever-present Uruguay had strong claims to the title, but the general feeling was that the 'vibe' was all about Europe.

The opening match between title-holders Brazil and Yugoslavia was played in torrential rain and ended in a tedious 0–0 draw. Gee whiz ... who'd have thought? Group One began with West Germany struggling to a poor quality 1–0 win over Chile. The East Germans beat Australia 2–0, but it was a game that the Aussies could easily have drawn. West Germany then defeated those marvellous boys from down-under 3–0, but the German fans were far from impressed by the manner of the victory, and booed and chanted continuously throughout the match. The fans' response didn't please West German captain Franz Beckenbauer, who made his feelings abundantly clear by flashing his bum or 'brown-eyeing' the vocal crowd during the match. And this was from Germany's legend of the game. To understand the significance in an Australian context, think of Don Bradman 'brown-eyeing' the members' stand during the Bodyline series. Anyway, Australia managed a 0–0 draw with Chile in another downpour, and the Germans (both East and West) marched on to the second round.

Group Two saw Brazil and Yugoslavia progress, but this Brazil bore little or no resemblance to previous Brazilian teams. They drew 0–0 with Yugoslavia and Scotland, and managed three goals against tiny Zaire. They seemed to have nothing in attack, and in general play they relied upon cynical, defensive fouling — tactics that belong to lesser teams. In the spirit of innovation that was sweeping the World Cup, Zaire managed a dubious first in their debut at the finals when Ernst Jean-Joseph recorded the first-ever positive drug test at a World Cup.

Group Three featured Holland, and the Dutchmen didn't disappoint. Like Brazil four years earlier, they were playing the game at a completely different level. They dazzled Uruguay 2–0; drew

0–0 with Sweden, dominating everything except the scoreboard; and finished off the group stage by thumping Bulgaria 4–1. The Swedes joined them in the second round. Group Four saw the hapless Italians forced to come from behind to beat Haiti 3–1, then draw with Argentina, and lose to Poland. As in all previous World Cups when they had failed to make the finals, this failure saw them stoned and pelted with fruit on departure, and then again upon arrival in Italy — mamma mia! The bookies seemed to have got the group pretty much right, as Poland and Argentina went on to the next round.

For the first time at a World Cup final, the second round would be another group stage, rather than a series of elimination games. The eight teams to have progressed this far were drawn into two groups of four, with each team playing all the others in their group. Cynics suggested that the new format was simply to provide more games that would in turn generate more revenue.

Now the Dutch took centre stage, and they began the show by demolishing a very strong Argentine side 4–0. They didn't just beat them; they crucified them with a dazzling combination of flair, skill, and panache. Next came the supremely fit East Germany: no problem, a 2–0 win, and they didn't even raise a sweat. Their final game in the group stage was against Brazil. In the nastiest game played since the Battle of Santiago, the Brazilians attacked the Dutch all over the field, with or without the ball. Despite wearing long hair and love beads, Holland were not going to be intimidated, and gave as good as they got ... and then some. They also scored two goals to nil, to win the group; Brazil (stricken with their identity crisis) finished second.

In the second group, West Germany accounted for their perennial whipping-boy Yugoslavia, 2–0, while the Lato-led Poland beat the Swedes 1–0 in yet another downpour. The weather was becoming as strange and destructive as the Brazilians, and in the next match it effectively took Sweden out of the match as the heavens opened with West Germany leading 4–2 just as the Swedes looked set to stage a comeback. Yugoslavia lost both of their remaining games, to Sweden and Poland 2–1, to set up the final group game between Poland and West Germany to determine who would meet the Dutchmen in the final. Again a torrential downpour ruined the match, and if the tournament officials' top priority had been World Cup-standard football this game (along with the Australia vs. Chile match) would have been postponed. Welcome to the wonderful world of television programming. West Germany got home, thanks almost entirely to their great keeper Sepp Maier.

The final pitted two of the fiercest rivals in Europe against each other — and we're not just talking sport here. To say that the Dutch and the Germans don't like each other is like saying that the sun is quite warm and a little more than a short, brisk walk away. To add a little spice to the usual rivalries between neighbouring countries, don't forget that Germany had twice occupied Holland during World Wars I and II. The final began as all matches do — with a kick-off. Sixteen passes and eighteen seconds later, the Dutch captain Cruyff found himself prostrate in the German goal area, having been fouled by Bertie Vogts. The referee awarded a penalty, Johan Neeskens scored for the Dutchmen, and the West Germans got their first touch of the ball for the match when they retrieved it from the back of the net. 1–0 to Holland.

Within two minutes of the start of the final, the Dutch had apparently achieved their ambition: they had humiliated their hated rival on the largest stage in the world. The only problem was that they still had another eighty-eight minutes to play. As Dutch defender Rudd Krol was later to remark: 'You can score too soon — we thought we had won but we forgot about the game until it was too late'. Holland's game-plan was based on the unified style of 'total football', which required each player to adapt and combine to suit the demands of the team. Thinking they had won the championship already, they lost their unified direction: some played conservatively to protect the lead, some over elaborated to further taunt the Germans, and Cruyff spent the entire match arguing with English referee Jack Taylor. Later it would emerge that the tactic of Cruyff being peripheral to the team structure was quite deliberate and indeed a tactic with some merit, as in a recent game against Bayern Munich (the de facto West German national team, give or take a player or two) Ajax had used this idea and won 6–0. However, the 1974 World Cup final was a different matter: the Dutch failed to score again while West Germany scored twice, through Breitner from the penalty spot and Gerd Muller, who scored his fourteenth World Cup goal to become the leading scorer in World Cup history.

As was the case with Brazil in 1950 and Hungary in 1954, the best team had not emerged triumphant. Later, in a good healthy case of sour grapes, Cruyff would say: 'The Germans didn't win the World Cup, we lost it'. You got that right! But let's not deny West Germany, who were a great side that had been building momentum since 1966. They were worthy finalists; it's just that in 1974 they were also the greatest party-poopers in the world. The Dutch had played like a beautiful dream: like Brazil and Hungary before them, they were loved by all as they epitomised the finest that the game has to offer. But, in many ways, football can be synonymous with cruelty — as we were about to find out.

Argentina 1978

Missing in action … only a fool gets bit by the same dog twice … something's fishy at the Estadio Rosario

Argentina was granted the honour of hosting World Cup eleven, which immediately threw the chances of a successful tournament into jeopardy. Like much of South America in the 1970s, Argentina was ruled by a brutal military government, and France, Holland, and Sweden in particular were keen to organise a boycott of the tournament by the entire contingent of European nations. They applied massive pressure to the new FIFA president, Brazilian Joao Havelange to force him to change the venue, but he refused to give in to the lobbying. As a result, arguably the best player in the world, Dutchman Johann Cruyff, withdrew from Holland's team in protest, and once again politics was exerting an influence on the World Cup before a ball had been kicked.

Other notable absentees when the final sixteen teams assembled were the Soviet Union, Yugoslavia and, for the third time in a row, England. Whether or not the English side had the talent or skill to succeed in the finals was almost irrelevant. The real point in mentioning their consistent failure is to highlight the clear pattern that was emerging. In 1970, Sir Alf Ramsey had said that English players were playing too many matches in a season. In 1974, in answer to a journalist's question about England's chances of winning a second World Cup, Johann Cruyff replied that England would never win a major tournament while they played so much domestic football — a sentiment echoed by out-going England manager Don Revie after their failure to qualify in 1978.

Group One consisted of a very good Italian side; a clever French team who were beginning to exhibit the skills of the soon-to-be legendary Michel Platini; the hosts, Argentina; and Hungary. Group Two had the ageing Polish squad from 1974, still under the guidance of Lato, and featuring another master in the making in Zbigniew Boniek; Tunisia (the sole representative from Africa); perennial bridesmaid Mexico; and a West German team who, without Franz Beckenbauer (now earning good money playing for the New York Cosmos) and Gerd Muller, looked a shadow of the great teams of 1972 and 1974. In Group Three, Brazil had a new coach in Coutinho — a man reputed to be willing and able to complicate a glass of water. Not only was he overly theoretical but he was a devotee of the more physical 'European' style that Brazil had so strangely and fruitlessly adopted in 1974. Sweden looked like a good bet to make the second round, but that was as much as anyone was prepared to guess. Spain were an almost completely unknown quantity, and Austria made up the numbers.

Group Four contained the Dutch maestros of 1974, minus their conductor Cruyff. As with much in the great man's life, the real reason for his absence from the tournament was the subject of wild speculation, with rumours including a mysterious break-in in at his Barcelona apartment and the more mundane theory that he was simply holding out for more money. However, the reason given most often, and importantly the reason given by Cruyff himself, was his boycott of the Argentine military dictators as host. Iran had qualified by defeating the Socceroos, adding to the increasingly exotic air of the tournament. Peru, with Teofilio Cubillas at the helm, looked every bit as likely as they had under very similar cir-cumstances in 1970. The sixteenth team was Scotland, who arrived brimming with confidence and attitude despite having played like a dead dog in the lead-up to the finals.

The tournament opened with (surprise, surprise) a dull, goalless draw between West Germany and Poland. The match was so bad, in fact, that it has since been declared the worst in World Cup history — way to go, fellas! The next day saw history made again when Tunisa defeated Mexico 3–1 and recorded the first victory by an African nation at the World Cup. Unfortunately, the Tunisians of 1978 are more often remembered for their involvement in a very iffy, goalless draw with a cunning West Germany who, having already guaranteed their progress to the second round, tried demonstrably not to score, in order to avoid Brazil or Argentina in the next round. They succeeded, leaving Poland as the other qualifier from Group Two to face the South American music.

Group One got off to a flyer with Italy, starring Paolo Rossi, beating France 2–1 in an open and exciting game. Argentina came from behind to beat Hungary 2–1, and then beat France in their next match. Italy defeated Hungary 3–1 to set up an intriguing battle with the hosts, which the *Azzurri* won by a single goal. Italy and Argentina qualified. In Group Three, Austria and Brazil got through, but neither looked convincing. Not for the first time, the Spanish choked on the big stage, while the Swedes just didn't have what it takes.

Group Four saw Peru and Holland progress, but the real story was Scotland. The Scots had arrived without any doubts about their own ability, but immediately crashed to a dreadful 3–1 loss to Peru. To make matters worse, Scottish winger Willy Johnston tested positive for pep pills — a fan remarked that Johnston's performance was the sort that gave pep pills a bad name. Things went rapidly from bad to worse when they put in an even more abysmal performance and drew 1–1 with Iran. Going into the final match against Holland, the Scots needed to win 3–0 in order to qualify.

A journalist from Holland asked the Dutch keeper, Jongbloed, if he thought Scotland could score three times. 'Yes', he replied, 'but not in one game'. As if on cue, the Scots did in fact score the three goals they needed but also conceded two to their opponents, so Holland and Peru went into the next round.

The tournament followed the model introduced in 1974, and the second round was organised as another group playoff. Group A, an all-European affair, was a shocker. Based on their form in the preliminary rounds, Italy had been installed as tournament favourite, but they began the second group stage struggling to a 0–0 draw against a colourless West Germany who had now managed a solitary goal in four matches. The Dutchmen smashed Austria 5–1, and then met their arch-rivals West Germany who, uncharacteristically, scored first and went ahead twice during the game, only to see Holland twice come back to draw 2–2. Italy's early brilliance was fading as they managed an unconvincing 1–0 victory over Austria. The Austrians then re-wrote both the form guide and the history books when they beat their neighbour West Germany for the first time in five decades, 3–2, and in so doing eliminated both teams from the tournament. In the group's final game, the Dutch again fell behind early to Italy, and again came from behind to win 2–1 and reach their second consecutive World Cup final.

The stage was set early in Group B when, in the first round of matches, Brazil swept aside Peru 3–0 and Argentina beat Poland 2–0 to re-ignite the fiercest rivalry in South American football. As if to confirm that they had been relegated to a side-show, Peru played like a team who had lost interest completely, and lost to Poland 1–0; on the main stage, Argentina and Brazil played out a tense nil-all draw. Brazil then beat Poland 3–1 to set Argentina a near-impossible task: to win the group and qualify for the final against Holland they had to defeat Peru 4–0 or 5–1. Immediately a strong rumour began to circulate that the Peruvian goalkeeper, 'El Loco' Quiroga, who was a naturalised Argentine, had been bribed to throw the game. Peru had nothing to play for, and Quiroga's performance against Poland certainly appeared as though he was establishing the grounds for an insanity plea. The rumours were never substantiated, but Argentina won 6–0 in a game that many South American fans and journalists still regard as highly suspicious.

The World Cup final would again feature the host nation against a representative of the 'other' continent. The match itself was an unusual mix of brutal fouling with occasional bouts of brilliant, attacking football by both sides. Chances were missed at both ends of the park before Kempes scored for Argentina. The Dutch hammered away in a nail-biting second half until, with eight minutes left in the match, Van der Kerkhof crossed to Nanninga, who headed the ball home. With the scores level, and in the final minutes of normal time, Krol put Reisenbrink through with a perfect long ball. Reisenbrink beat the keeper but hit the post: extra time.

As soon as Reisenbrink's shot hit the post, everyone knew that the Dutchmen would fail again; somehow, the sense of doom was almost palpable. Argentina rallied and scored two goals in extra time to seal the victory 3–1. Once again, the Dutch had been denied, only this time it seemed doubly unjust as not only would they have been worthy winners in 1978, but some form of consolation for their failure in 1974 seemed long overdue. However, the World Cup had returned to South America. For a short time, Argentina could celebrate victory and forget about the mothers of the 'disappeared', who came every day to the plaza in Buenos Aires to petition silently for justice for their sons and daughters.

Spain 1982

Paolo Rossi: the return of the grievous angel ... the foul of the century ... Brazil: a tragedy in two acts

The twelfth World Cup, held in Spain in 1982, was, if nothing else, a tremendous yardstick of the growth in popularity of the beautiful game. FIFA president Joao Havelange had secured the necessary votes for his election by making promises to many third world nations about increasing their opportunities to appear at the greatest show on earth. Now it was payday, and Havelange *el Presidente* was as good as his word. Spain '82 would feature twenty-four finalists instead of the previous limit of sixteen. This not only satisfied his pre-election markers but also accommodated the ever-increasing demands of that bottomless pit known as television. Put simply, more games make for more viewing hours, more hours sell more advertising, and more advertising equals *mucho dinero — si senor!*

As was the case in Argentina four years earlier, there was no obvious pre-tournament favourite; rather, many teams had solid claims on the title. France, with the now completely brilliant Michel Platini, looked good. West Germany, which included Karl Heinz Rummenigge and a young Pierre Littbarski, would, as always, be there or thereabouts. The hosts, Spain, were also rated a good chance in the official form guide; however, privately, many pundits suggested that, as they had choked at every other tournament away from home, nothing short of a tracheotomy would get them to a final in front of their home crowd. The Italians were

said to have an outstanding defence, but struggled to score goals —
as Yogi Berra might say: 'It's deja vu all over again.' These four had
the best credentials of the European challengers; the team most
notable by their absence was Holland, who had inevitably come to
the end of an era but had not yet begun the next.

From South America there were two main contenders: the
title-holders, Argentina, and … go on, have a guess … no, really,
you can do it. You need a hint? — okay, it starts with a B.
BRAZIL!? — well done, jolly good show. Argentina, still under
the guidance of 'the wig', Senor Menotti, sported essentially the
same squad as in 1978 plus one new team member: Diego
Maradonna, who had just joined Spanish club Barcelona for a
world-record US$8.8 million. The Brazilians had changed
coaches: Coutinho and his Euro-style, physical game plan had been
replaced with Santana and a return to the philosophy of *jogo bonito*.
Zico, Socrates, and Falcao were the key players in this welcome
return to the 'samba' style of Brazilian football that had brought
so much success and the admiration of the football world. Artist
Joan Miro created the best World Cup poster of all time for the
tournament, and FIFA made their own creative contribution with
the introduction of the penalty shoot-out.

And so to the group stage of Spain 1982:

Group One
Italy, Poland,
Cameroon, Peru

Group Two
West Germany, Chile,
Algeria, Austria

Group Three
Argentina, Belgium,
Hungary, El Salvador

Group Four
England, France,
Kuwait, Czechoslovakia

Group Five
Spain, Northern Ireland,
Honduras, Yugoslavia

Group Six
Brazil, New Zealand,
Scotland, USSR

The opening game, between Argentina and Belgium, was remarkable for two reasons. One, the Belgians had clearly been watching a lot of Bruce Lee movies as a part of their preparation for the tournament, and they treated their opponents to an impromptu re-enactment of *Enter the Dragon*. Understandably, this upset the Argentines and in particular Maradonna, who was the primary target; it upset the commentators; and it even upset the fans watching in the stadium. In fact, the only person who seemed untroubled by the Belgian tactics was referee Christov, who probably went on to found the first Extreme Sports TV network. Secondly, for the first time in twenty coma-inducing years, the opening game produced a goal: Belgium 1, Argentina 0.

Hungary then completed the first round of Group Three matches with a hard-fought 10–1 victory over noble El Salvador. Argentina regrouped and smashed Hungary 4–1, while all-conquering Belgium continued on their winning way with an emphatic 1–0 landslide over noble El Salvador. Belgium and Hungary then drew 1–1, Argentina beat the noble El Salvador 2–0, and the group was complete. Belgium and Argentina qualified for the next round — who'd be a punter?

Group One saw Italy and Poland progress. The Italians scored only two goals for the entire group stage, and were criticised to within an inch of their lives. In an act of pure self-preservation they stopped talking to the press about football: music, ballet, politics, the weather … anything but football. All football enquiries from the media were referred to captain Dino Zoff, who had last spoken publicly shortly after Nero's famous violin recital. Cameroon were thrilling, but went home; Poland were not, and went through to the next stage.

Group Two provided the first of several upsets when Algeria beat West Germany 2–1 in the first game. For the rest of the group stage, the Germans were methodical to the point of disbelief, especially in their next match when they crushed Chile 4–1, thanks to a hat-trick from Rummenigge. The results in the group panned out so that in the final game West Germany would meet neighbour Austria, with both teams knowing that a 1–0 victory to the Germans would ensure that they both progressed to round two. West Germany scored after ten minutes and then both sides played kick-to-kick for eighty minutes, making no further attempt to score. Protests were lodged and appeals for the expulsion of both teams were made; but, to its eternal shame, FIFA allowed the result to stand. The German's reputation had sunk to depths not seen since the mid-1940s.

Group Four saw England and France qualify ahead of Czechoslovakia and the plucky Kuwaitis. In the opening match, Brian Robson scored the fastest goal in World Cup history (in the first minute of play) as England defeated the highly fancied Frenchmen 3–1. Could this signal the re-emergence of English football, long in decline since the heartbreaking loss in 1970?

Group Five provided another huge shock when debutant Honduras held Spain to a 1–1 draw and then punished the sceptics when they repeated the result against fellow flyweight Northern Ireland. But in another example of poignant football cruelty, Yugoslavia recorded their only victory in the final match against Honduras to eliminate them both from the tournament. Meanwhile, Northern Ireland, who featured the youngest player in World Cup history, in Manchester United's Norman Whiteside, accounted for Spain 1–0, and secured a berth for both of them in the next round.

Brazil cut through Group Six like a band-saw with ten goals and three victories to send a shiver through their rivals. Zico was especially destructive, with two goals and two assists, against New Zealand. They were joined in the second round by the USSR, who overcame perennially disappointing Scotland and debutants (at Australia's expense) New Zealand.

The second phase of World Cup 1982 was organised as another group stage: four groups of three teams, with the winners going into the semi-finals.

Group A	**Group B**
Poland, Belgium, USSR	West Germany, England, Spain
Group C	**Group D**
Brazil, Italy, Argentina	France, Austria, Northern Ireland

You want to talk 'group of death'? Group C remains the toughest group in recorded history, and winning it would prove to be a beyond-death experience. Not even the *Tibetan Book of the Dead* explains how to qualify from a group featuring Brazil, Argentina, and Italy.

The World Cup tournament has an uncanny knack of becoming a stage for events that take on a significance well beyond football. In the final match in Group A, after both teams had managed to defeat Belgium, the Polish team were pitted against the USSR for a place in the semi-finals. In Poland, confrontation between the Solidarity movement led by Lech Walesa and the Soviet-backed communist government was reaching a critical point. Barely six months before the tournament, under threat of a Soviet invasion, the Polish government had declared martial law in an attempt to crack down on strikes and demonstrations. Paramilitary riot police had shot and killed protestors, and persecution of Solidarity members was rife. In this atmosphere, the two teams met with Poland, ahead on goal difference thanks to a Boniek hat-trick against Belgium, only needing a 0–0 draw to qualify.

The Poles turned the match into a piece of Brechtian political theatre — controlling play, they would dribble the ball to the corner flag and hold it there for what seemed like ninety minutes. Some were outraged, but most of the world applauded. The German/Austrian debacle had been nothing more than self-serving match-fixing; this was about matters greater than sport. Poland eliminated the USSR to progress to the semi-finals.

In Group B, England were missing injured striker Kevin Keegan, and their inability to score in either of their second-round matches saw West Germany go through, courtesy of a 2–1 victory over Spain. The Germans had been solid rather than inspirational; but with Littbarski, Fischer, and Rummenigge combining beautifully, they looked potent enough to go all the way.

Italy had begun their journey at World Cup '82 like a dog with two broken legs — their defence was unbelievable, their attack was indefinable. Coach Bearzot had pinned all his goal-scoring hopes on Paolo Rossi. Four years earlier, Rossi had been the new sensation of Serie A; however, since 1978, the striker's status in football had headed south thanks to persistent knee injuries and club failure. Things hit rock-bottom in 1980 when he was suspended for his part in a match-fixing scandal; and, coming into the tournament in Spain, he had not played for two years. Rossi failed to score in any of the initial group matches, and journalists described him as a ghost, aimlessly wandering the pitch. With each game in which the Italian offence failed, the pressure on Bearzot grew; but still he backed Rossi.

In the opening match of Group C, Italy met Argentina. Three men decided this game: Italian defender Claudio Gentile, Argentine striker Diego Maradona, and Romanian referee Nicolai Rainea. Gentile played in such a manner that he could easily have been charged with aggravated assault, if not attempted murder. He didn't need to change shirts with Maradona after the game as he had already torn two of them off his back by half-time. Referee Rainea found nothing wrong with this. Finally, after another in a series of life-threatening tackles by Gentile on Maradona, the referee produced a yellow card — for Maradona. He would eventually yellow-card the Italian defender as well (one of five yellow and one red cards for the match), but the damage had been done. Having stymied the Argentine ace, Italy managed to score twice through Tardelli and Cabrini to win the game 2–1. Rossi's only contribution was one of the yellow cards.

In the next match, Brazil beat the world-weary Argentina 3–1. After suffering at the hands (and boots) of defenders throughout the tournament and watching his tormentors go unpunished, Maradona finally snapped and was sent off for kicking Batista in the groin. It was a disgraceful foul, but in the light of how he had been treated it was a moment of perverse irony to see the little Argentine striker's tournament end this way.

Now it was high noon at the OK Corral, and you could almost hear Sergio Leone playing in the background as Brazil and Italy faced each other for a place in the semi-finals. Brazil were unbackable favourites and were rightly considered to be possibly the greatest Brazil side ever — even better than the Brazil of 1970. Rossi had not been able to trouble the scorer now in four appearances, but still Bearzot selected him to start.

The match was played in an atmosphere of almost unbearable tension, and it remains one of the greatest games in World Cup history. Gentile marked Brazilian match-winner Zico: bye-bye Zico. Finally, Rossi repaid his coach's faith, and in the fifth minute of play he scored to give the *Azzurri* a precious 1–0 lead. Brazil struck back almost immediately, through captain Socrates, to level the scores at 1–1; but Rossi refused to be outdone, and he banged home a second to restore his team's lead after twenty-five minutes. The game was a classic clash of styles, with the Brazilians controlling the ball through stylish, attacking play while the Italians were content to try and contain their opponents and strike on the counter-attack. With Gentile and Cabrini restricting the Brazilian's ability to score, the two sides went in at half-time with Italy leading 2–1.

Twenty-three minutes into the second half, Falcao scored to equalise again for Brazil; but, if anything, their all-out attack looked to be faltering as they consistently created chances that they weren't able to finish. Still, with a superior goal difference to Italy, a draw would have been good enough for the South Americans to make the semi-final. The Italians refused to give in and persisted with their counter-attacking game, searching for a winning goal. Then, with only a quarter of an hour left to play, the Brazilian defence failed to clear the ball properly from their area after an Italian corner. The ball spilled to the top of the box and Paolo Rossi drilled it into the back of the net to give his team victory, 3–2, and to complete his return from the wilderness.

After the political drama of Group A and the personal melo-drama and classic football of Group C, the final qualification group was a little pedestrian, but you can't have it all. France did enough to beat Austria, 1–0, and then destroyed Northern Ireland, 4–1, thanks to a double from Dominique Rocheteau, to book their place in the semi-finals. So the semi-finals of Spain '82 were to be an all-European affair: Italy vs Poland, and West Germany vs France.

Rossi's change in form was a revelation for the Italian team: his first goal against Brazil had seemingly exorcised a demon from himself and from the Italian side as a whole, and now he simply couldn't stop scoring. In the semi-final in Barcelona, he knocked in one in each half to secure an easy, 2–0, victory over Poland, who were without their suspended match-winner Boniek. Rossi now had five goals in two matches, and Bearzot couldn't stop grinning.

Meanwhile, in Seville, France and West Germany played out one of the most dramatic and controversial matches in the history of the sport. If Poland vs the USSR was Brechtian drama, this played out like something out of a story by Franz Kafka. West Germany began the match with injured star Rummenigge on the bench, but winger Pierre Littbarski stepped into his shoes with ease and gave the Germans a 1–0 lead after seventeen minutes. The French had started slowly, but their opponents' goal seemed to spur them into action: nine minutes later, Michel Platini scored from the penalty spot to equalise. Now the game settled into a tense routine of thrust and parry, with neither team able to cut through the other's defence. Midway through the second half, the French split the Germans wide open with a long through-ball to put Patrick Battiston one-on-one with goalkeeper Tony Schumacher. With Battiston bearing down on goal, Schumacher proceeded to commit what is now known as 'the foul of the century' — racing off his line, he made no attempt to play the ball but instead took the Frenchman out with an Aussie Rules style shirt-front, capped off with a flying elbow to the face. Battiston was knocked unconscious and lost two teeth, and play was stopped for ten minutes while he was stretchered from the ground. Amazingly, Dutch referee Charles Corver awarded a goal kick, when a red card plus a penalty would have been insufficient punishment for the violence of the goalkeeper's attack.

The bizarre foul and the referee's strange failure to do anything about it seemed to cast a spell over players of both teams, and at full-time the scores were still locked at 1–1. As the game went into extra time, the French team, sparked by the genius of Platini, regained their composure quickly and scored within minutes of the re-start through a volley from sweeper Marius Tresor. *Les Bleus* now looked absolutely irresistible, and within six minutes they had added a third goal, to lead 3–1 deep into extra time. West Germany needed a minor miracle, and they turned to their match-winner Rummenigge who, despite being injured, came off the bench to score almost immediately and restore a glimmer of hope for the Germans. And then, just in case anyone in the grandstand was getting bored with a game that had already included five goals (three of them in extra time), a near-homicidal foul, and a blind, deaf, and dumb referee, Klaus Fischer, left unattended by the French defenders, rattled home a bicycle-kick goal, to equalise at 3–3 and send the game to a penalty shoot-out for the first time in World Cup history.

Have I mentioned that football can be a cruel game? If this was ever in doubt it was rammed home during the penalty shoot-out as the French team faltered under the intense pressure, and the West German goalkeeper, who by rights should have been cooling his heels in a Spanish jail cell, emerged as the hero of the day. Schumacher saved two penalties to eliminate the French, who had delighted all with the elegant football of Platini, and send his team into the final. Even neutrals wept with outrage at this nauseating miscarriage of justice.

As the Italian side prepared to meet West Germany in the final, they found themselves in a situation they had never encountered before and probably never will again. The whole world (with the possible exceptions of Maradona, Zico, and a handful of towns in Bavaria) wanted them to win. All of a sudden, a man like Gentile had become a source of hope, inspiration, and justice — in the style of Judge Dread. Maybe he would maim Schumacher? … here's hoping.

The Italians began cautiously, and their first real chance on goal came in the twenty-fifth minute when they won a penalty which, somehow, Cabrini missed. After the extraordinary drama of the semi-final and the Italy vs Brazil match, the final was shaping as an anti-climax, and at half-time the two teams went in at 0–0. Much like in 1970, when the Italians left their best game in the semi-final, an exhausted West Germany were beginning to falter. The second half saw the Italians open the game up and, after twenty minutes, their talisman Rossi finally scored. A second goal, from Marco Tardelli, came ten minutes later, and he finished it with the most heart-felt goal celebration that I have ever seen. To seal the victory, Altobelli scored a third goal, and even a late consolation to West Germany's Paul Breitner could do nothing to take the gloss off the Italian triumph. Among a team of heroes, none was greater than Scirea at the heart of the Italian defence. Italy had won 3–1, and collected their third World Cup trophy to equal the Brazilian's record. A final wave, and it was ciao baby and on to Mexico '86.

Mexico 1986

Rising from the rubble … Day of the dead for *jogo bonito* … Maradona: the hand of god …

The thirteenth World Cup, in 1986, was eventually hosted by Mexico for an unprecedented second time, but for a while it was threatened by a unique kind of double jeopardy. The original hosts, Columbia, were forced to withdraw when they realised in 1982 that they couldn't afford to stage the party. The Columbian infrastructure could cope with a tournament of sixteen teams (just), but the increase to twenty-four teams would be too much for them to bear. The tournament was now bigger than the Olympics and could generate enormous revenue if properly managed, and the announcement of Mexico as the new hosts was met with the usual allegations of bribed officials and a corrupt process from the unsuccessful applicants. After the Columbian false start, the chances of the new hosts running a successful tournament were threatened when, in September 1985, an earthquake measuring 8.1 on the Richter scale hit Mexico City. With nearly ten thousand killed or seriously injured and thirty thousand homeless, it evoked memories of Chile in 1962; but as none of the stadiums were damaged, Mexico went ahead with its preparations.

Going into the tournament, four teams stood out as real title contenders: Argentina, West Germany, France, and … wait, don't tell me … Brazil? Yes, amazing. How does he do it?

Argentina under coach Bilardo and featuring the now rampant, mature version of Maradonna at the absolute peak of his career, looked great. They had been mugged in 1982 in their opening game against Belgium and had not recovered. This time they would be ready. West Germany had proved that whether their side was brilliant, adequate, or crap they were still guaranteed a place in the semi-finals. In '82, with a pretty ordinary side, for the most part, they had reached the final. The 1986 vintage, with Rudi Voeller up front, Pierre Littbarski on the wing, and 'the kaiser' Franz Beckenbauer at the helm, looked very dangerous. Added to these familiar faces was a new one that the world was soon to get to know well: Lothar Matthaus.

The French and the Brazilians had a remarkably similar story to tell. Both were brilliant, attacking sides and had been extremely unlucky to be knocked out in '82. Both returned to the World Cup looking stronger again: France, led by midfield genius Michel Platini at the peak of his powers, had won the European championship just two years earlier, while Brazil were still based around the accomplished core of Socrates, Zico, Falcao, and Junior, but now also featured Careca up front. Against Italy in '82, they would have won by three goals if they'd had a finisher (like Rossi) of Careca's quality.

The Italians had gone into a decline and were now, officially, crap; the hosts, Mexico, had no chance; and the Dutch hadn't even qualified. The finalists for 1986 were:

Group One
Italy, Argentina,
Bulgaria, South Korea

Group Two
Mexico, Belgium,
Paraguay, Iraq

Group Three
France, USSR,
Hungary, Canada

Group Four
Brazil, Spain, Algeria,
Northern Ireland

Group Five
Denmark, West Germany,
Scotland, Uruguay

Group Six
England, Portugal,
Poland, Morocco

The tournament kicked off with Italy vs Bulgaria and, even as opening matches go, it was a stinker. At half-time I couldn't help wondering if, in the interests of public safety, it should be accompanied by a warning against operating heavy machinery while under the influence of this game. Leading 1–0 with only a few minutes remaining, the Italians lulled themselves into unconsciousness and Bulgaria equalised.

Thankfully for the reputation of the game, the next match saw Brazil meet Spain. The Brazilians won a pulsating contest 1–0, but Spain had an apparently good goal disallowed by Australian referee Chris Bainbridge. In the end, though, the injustice of the disallowed goal was mitigated when both Brazil and Spain qualified from Group Four.

In Group One, Argentina, Italy, and Bulgaria qualified for the next round; the latter by being one of the four best third-place-getters. Argentina, and in particular Maradona, who had either scored or created just about all of their first-round goals, looked the business; Italy seemed to lack any real self-belief; and Bulgaria were making up the numbers. Group Two featured the hosts, who got off to a flying start with a 2–1 win over a faltering Belgium. Mexico, Paraguay, and Belgium progressed, but none of them looked likely to do anything beyond the second round — which just goes to show that looks can be deceiving.

Group Three featured one of the pre-tournament favourites in France; but, after the completion of the group stage, all the talk was about the USSR, who had knocked in nine goals in three games (including six against Hungary). Who could possibly beat them? In Rats, Belanov, and Aleinikov they had players with the usual high degree of technique and organisation that characterised Soviet football, but they also had something typically lacking in the Eastern-bloc philosophy: flair. These guys played at breakneck speed and specialised in cracking twenty-five-metre shots that actually went in. They looked as irresistible as the Dutch had in 1974. Both France and the USSR qualified fairly easily.

Group Five was the tournament's 'group of death', but was also remarkable for a couple of other reasons. It featured the debut of Denmark at the World Cup, and the debutants dazzled everyone with their exhilarating play. It also featured a Uruguayan side that seemed determined to establish its reputation as the dirtiest and most vicious side to have competed in a World Cup. By the end of the third-group match against Scotland, they had collected two red cards, innumerable yellows, and set a record for the fastest send-off in World Cup history, after 56 seconds of play against the Scots — hats off to Jose Batista! Their approach to the whole tournament was considered so appalling that they were fined $100,000 for their general attitude, a punishment that has never been seen before or since.

The positive counter-balance to Uruguay's performance was the revelation of the Danes. In Elkjær-Larsen, Arnesen, and Olsen they had gifted, attacking players who seemed able to score at will — and, with a lazy six against Uruguay and two against West Germany, score they did. West Germany looked dull but capable, and qualified alongside Denmark and Uruguay.

Meanwhile, in Group Six, things were threatening to disintegrate on a number of fronts. England were just too awful to be true, losing 1–0 to a Portuguese team who had almost refused to take the field due to a pay dispute. They followed this up with a goalless draw against Morocco. On the verge of elimination, Gary Lineker found his touch and bagged a hat-trick inside forty minutes against Poland to get England through to round two, along with surprise-packet Morocco and a strangely unconvincing Poland.

The second round of matches would be sudden death for the losers. The fixture looked like this:

Mexico vs Bulgara	Belgium vs USSR
Brazil vs Poland	Argentina vs Uruguay
France vs Italy	West Germany vs Morocco
England vs Paraguay	Spain vs Denmark

The Denmark vs Spain, France vs Italy, and Argentina vs Uruguay matches looked to be the pick of the card while Belgium, Poland, and Morocco were dealt the toughest hands. The hosts began with a straightforward 2–0 win over Bulgaria, who bowed out of the tournament maintaining their record of sixteen World Cup matches without a win. Next up was Belgium vs USSR — a mere formality in the most people's minds, including the Belgians themselves, who were so sure of losing to the rampaging Soviets that they hadn't even bothered to book accommodation beyond that night. In a match that I rate as the greatest World Cup game of all time, the plucky Belgians twice came from behind to take the game into extra time, during which they clinched the sweetest of victories, 4–3. But more of this later.

Brazil reminded everyone that the Soviets' astonishing elimination didn't mean you could throw the form guide out the window when they smashed a thoroughly dispirited Poland, 4–0. Argentina, wary of their old foes Uruguay, manufactured a satisfactory 1–0 win, but again the focus of everything seemed to be Maradona. Interestingly enough, the Uruguayans, putting aside their disgraceful defending and spiteful tactics, played the sort of cultured football they were capable of, and pushed Argentina all the way.

France, led by Platini, humbled reigning world champion Italy 2–0, and showed everybody that they were just getting into their stride. At the other end of the spectrum, West Germany scraped home unconvincingly 1–0 over Morocco in a performance that defied description. England slaughtered Paraguay 3–0, thanks again to Gary Lineker, but failed to put to rest questions that lingered from their abysmal start to the tournament. In the final game of the second round, Spain came back after trailing 1–0 to annihilate first-round superstars Denmark, courtesy of four goals to Real Madrid's Butragueño. The Danes' brilliant cameo was over, and they left the tournament in humiliation.

The elimination of the USSR and Denmark had restored some sense of normality to the tournament: now that the wheat had been sorted from the chaff, the giants of world football would play for a place in the semi-finals. France vs Brazil was a true battle of the titans — surely this was the final the tournament deserved being played prematurely. Conversely, the two least-convincing survivors, West Germany and Mexico, would meet, meaning that one of them would progress to the semis. Argentina would meet the born-again Englishmen in a match played with the Falklands War as background. And, finally, giant-killing Belgium would take on the now-rampant Spaniards.

In Guadalajara, Brazil met France in a magnificent match that featured brilliant, attacking football played at the highest level by both teams. Brazil scored first through Careca, but Platini was able to equalise for *les Bleus* four minutes before half-time. The deadlock continued into the second half until, eighteen minutes before full-time, Zico was brought on as a substitute and almost immediately earned a penalty for his side. Zico stepped up to take the shot, despite the fact that he clearly had not yet warmed to the pace of the game, and his weak attempt was saved by French keeper Joel Batts. So, with the score locked at 1–1, the game went to extra time and then on to the dreaded penalty shoot-out. Finally France won 4–3, but not before both Platini and Socrates had missed their shots — pure heart-attack material.

Argentina and England met in Mexico City under a virtual state of siege, surrounded by police, soldiers, and even tanks. The war over the tiny Falkland Islands had raised tensions to unbearable levels and, like Poland vs USSR in 1982, the match had taken on qualities that transcended sport. The stage was set for history to be made, and onto it strode Diego Maradona. In a performance that seemed to encapsulate the extraordinary and infuriating contradiction that he was to become, he settled the match with two equally breathtaking goals. The first was a cunningly executed handball header (the infamous 'hand of God' goal) that fooled everyone except for the enraged English team; the second was simply the greatest individual goal ever scored at a World Cup, as he ran half the length of the pitch with the ball, beating seven bewildered Englishmen, before slotting it into the net.

Gary Lineker managed a consolation goal for England; but that was all, she wrote.

As if to offer some relief from the high drama, Mexico and West Germany played out a dull, goalless draw in Monterrey. The hosts now revealed their exit strategy for the tournament, promptly falling to pieces when the match went to penalties, and losing 4–1.

That left Belgium and Spain. The Spanish, perennial chokers on the big stage, looked as though they believed that this was their time. The Belgians had been as convincing in round one as a used-car salesman's promise, and had only got through thanks to the greatest of efforts against the Soviet Union. But such efforts can transform a team, and the now fire-proof Belgians started the quarter-final as they had finished against the USSR. For once, the Spaniards came to the party, and the two teams put on a breath-taking display of attacking football that ended 1–1 and was finally settled 5–4 on penalties, with Belgium taking the honours thanks to keeper extraordinaire Jean-Marie Pfaff.

The semi-finals pitted West Germany against France in a replay of the infamous 1982 semi-final. Exactly how the Germans had managed to get this far was a mystery to everyone. But one thing was certain, regardless of who their opponent was: they were always difficult to overcome. Revenge and a well-deserved place in the final was on offer for the French but, alas, they started badly, conceding a soft goal from an Andreas Brehme free kick after only nine minutes, The Germans battened down the hatches as the French attack came, but France were clearly showing the effects of their epic quarter-final against Brazil, and failed to make any impression on the German defence. After staunchly resisting for most of the game, Rudi Voeller scored a breakaway goal in the final minute of play to give the Germans a 2–0 victory. France were on their way home, again, and West Germany were into the final.

In the other semi, Belgium looked to reprise their role as David to the Argentine Goliath. The Belgians sat back in defence and absorbed Argentina's assault, hoping to catch them on the break through Clausen, their Olympic-speed striker. And the strategy was working. In the final few minutes of the first half, with the score locked at 0–0, Belgium twice put Clausens into space with just the keeper to beat. Both times the flag was raised for offside, and both times the decision looked highly dubious on the television replay. The Belgians had finally run out of luck. In the second half it was all Argentina as Maradona said to his teammates, 'Give me the ball, amigos' and scored twice to book a place with West Germany in the final.

To the surprise of everyone, the final was ultimately a close-run thing. The Germans started the game every bit as badly as they had played for the rest of the tournament while Argentina seemed to be running on cruise control. With all eyes on Maradona, Boca Juniors' defender Jose Luis Brown stepped up to score after twenty minutes; and when Valdano bagged a second goal ten minutes into the second half it looked like game over. But, finally, the Germans clicked into gear. Rudi Voeller, brought on as a substitute at the end of the first half, was starting to cause problems for the Argentine defence and, with fifteen minutes left to play, he created a great opportunity for Rummenigge, who finished nicely to restore some hope for West Germany at 2–1. Voeller was clearly the danger man, and he underlined this almost immediately when he scored to tie things up at 2–2 within ten minutes of full time. Could the unthinkable happen? No, senor! Almost immediately from the restart of play, Maradona tore a hole through the German defence to create a goal for Jorge Burruchaga, who obligingly banged it into the back of the net to seal Argentina's second World Cup.

Despite the early omens of catastrophe, the 1986 World Cup tournament had been a great success. It had seen a handful of great teams with an abundance of truly gifted individuals meet each other in open competition. It had served up three fabulous matches in Belgium vs USSR, France vs Brazil, and Belgium vs Spain. Morocco had made it into the second round, carrying the banner for African football, and the Danes and Soviets had taken the world by surprise with their displays of breathtaking football. There had been no shortage of drama and controversy; and, at the end of it all, one man rose above everything and everyone else to lift the Jules Rimet trophy. Clearly, the 1986 tournament ranks as one of the best ever staged — strangely, Mexico's other tournament in 1970 is also considered a candidate for 'best ever' for many of the same reasons.

Italy 1990

How far can too far go? … Roger Milla and the art of ageing gracefully … third time lucky for Lothar Matthäus

There are many stories about the origins of football. In fact, it would probably be easier to compile a list of countries that don't claim to be the birthplace of the game. Whether it's peasants throwing a piece of fruit through a hoop, warriors kicking around a severed head in a leather bag, or a five-thousand-year-old statue with a ball at its feet, the creation myths of football are as varied as they are plentiful. One of the more substantial claims is the fourteenth-century game of Calcio, played in Florence; although, if you ask me, it bears a far stronger resemblance to the 1975 film *Rollerball* than modern football. Still, it's real and played to this very day, and it forms the basis to Italy's boast to be 'the home of football' — and so it was to Italy that FIFA returned to host the fourteenth World Cup.

Hosting the World Cup tournament was no longer just a matter of national pride. Since 1970 it had become increasingly obvious that, if it was run properly, a truck-load of money could be had by all. Advertising, TV rights, ticket sales, and merchandise were all enormous sources of revenue. Despite beginning in the rubble of an earthquake and having TV communication problems that reduced coverage of the early games to a farce, Mexico 1986 had managed to generate a profit of nearly US$100 million. Countries that reached the latter stages of the tournament would receive payments of around US$2 million. Even Canada, who not only failed to win a match but hadn't even scored a single goal, went home from Mexico with slightly less than a cool million dollars for their trouble. This was the reality of the corporatisation of the sport, with no drug testing: it was a beast of unbelievable power and influence. Today, FIFA has more members than the United Nations, is wealthier than many countries, and can wield enough influence to change the course of political and social life in an entire region.

Italy wanted World Cup 1990 and, using everyone from the Pope to Pino the wonder horse to lobby FIFA, they got it. Most people didn't doubt that the Italians could stage a successful tournament; after all, they did it in 1934 and should have been able to do it again. However, there were some concerns that lingered around the international football community. Italy had the stadiums (nearly), the infrastructure (mostly), and the communications sophistication (most definitely). What concerned most of the doubters was security — not against Munich 1972-style terrorists, but a more insidious and only slightly less lethal threat: football hooligans. These people (I refuse to call them fans) had become a dreadful blight on the game and on society as a whole. There were versions of the beast in other places, but the problem was mainly European, with the worst offenders coming from England, the Netherlands, Germany, and Italy. They were numerous, beer-fuelled, aggressive, and highly organised, and in the late 1980s and early 1990s they left a trail of incredible chaos and destruction across western Europe. Still, the show must go on, and go on it did.

Qualification produced its usual supply of raised eyebrows. In Europe, two-time semi-finalist France and the wonderkids of 1986, Denmark, both missed out. In South America things got even funkier: Chile was disqualified in a match against Brazil because their goalkeeper faked being hit by a missile from the crowd. Mexico were also banned after playing over-age players in the World Youth Championship — *ay carumba*!

Those who made it past qualification and were allowed to come to the party were divided thus:

Group One
Italy, Austria, Czechoslovakia, USA

Group Two
Cameroon, Argentina, USSR, Romania

Group Three
Brazil, Costa Rica, Scotland, Sweden

Group Four
Colombia, West Germany, United Arab Emirates, Yugoslavia

Group Five
Belgium, South Korea, Spain, Uruguay.

Group Six
England, Holland, Republic of Ireland, Egypt

Groups Two, Four, and Six looked very tough. There were no clear-cut favourites so Italy, as hosts, found themselves installed as favourites by default. West Germany, beaten finalists from '86, looked a stronger, more cohesive unit than four years earlier; and the Dutch, reigning European champions with their AC Milan trio of Van Basten, Rijkaard, and Guullet, looked to be a real threat. Argentina's hopes were embodied in Maradona, who looked much the worse for wear, and another 'European-style' Brazil failed to convince anybody.

The opening game saw defending champions Argentina meet Cameroon. The attacking spirit of the Africans was a breath of fresh air, but their tackling took the idea of attack a little too far. Cameroon kicked the living crap out of Argentina, picked up three yellow cards and had two players sent off, but still won the match, 1–0. Argentina looked simply abominable, and based on their performance weren't capable of matching the USSR in their next game. The Soviets were a team in decline after having peaked in 1988 when they were beaten in the final of the European Championship by Holland, but they still looked good enough to beat this impotent Argentine team. They weren't — Argentina threw the form guide out the window and won 2–0. To further consolidate his reputation for cynical opportunism, Maradona hand-balled a Soviet shot on goal off the line, and again escaped punishment from the referee. Cameroon topped the group, but two red and seven yellow cards from three matches highlighted the problems inherent in their barbaric approach to defence. Somehow, Argentina and Romania qualified alongside them.

In Group One, the Italians had discovered a genuine secret weapon in super-sub Toto Schillaci. The Sicilian scored in Italian victories over Austria and Czechoslovakia, and in combination with the young Roberto Baggio and Gianluca Vialli formed an attack that looked capable of scoring enough goals to win the tournament. Unlike four years earlier, when they sparkled in patches but never as a whole, this side played with an all-round consistency that gave the home fans real hope. They qualified with three wins ahead of Czechoslovakia, whose first round highlight was a 5–1 drubbing of the USA.

Group Three saw Brazil and Costa Rica qualify, the shock elimination of Sweden in straight sets, and Scotland prove themselves a model of consistency in failing to survive the first round yet again. Brazil won all three first-round matches; but, under coach Lazaroni, they were unrecognisable except for their yellow shirts. 'No more *jogo bonito*, only sweat and sacrifice' said midfielder Dunga and, having been eliminated in the last two tournaments playing their trademark beautiful game, you could see where they were coming from. Nonetheless, this side was too pragmatic and the transformation was too radical. Despite their early form, the words of Pele rang in everyone's ears: 'When they meet a good team, they will lose'.

If the new-model Brazil was a disappointment, West Germany was a revelation. In '86 they had been fit, strong, and powerful, but about as inspiring as Frankfurt airport. This time, with Voller and Klinsmann up front, Haessler and Littbarski in the middle, and Matthaus and Brehme down back, they were simply awesome. With nine goals from just two games, including four against the fancied Yugoslavia, they showed everyone that they were the real deal and that, for once, they'd brought their goal-kicking boots. Yugoslavia and Colombia followed them through from Group Four, the latter courtesy of an unlikely draw against the German juggernaut.

Spain, Belgium, and Uruguay all qualified from Group Five, but all three looked soft and unconvincing. Each seemed vaguely reminiscent of the side they had been four years ago in Mexico, but they were pale imitations of the class of '86.

The final group was probably the toughest of the opening round. In addition to Holland, it featured an English team led by Sir Bobby Robson with the mercurial Paul Gascoigne providing a creative spark in the midfield, and a Republic of Ireland side which, under the guidance of Jack Charlton, was experiencing an extraordinary renaissance. Ireland had been lost until Saint Jack came along, He assembled a squad (sometimes using great-grandmothers as a pretext for player eligibility) and took them to Euro '88, where they proceeded to beat England for the first time in history. Using the long ball, hard running, and tough defence, they were a side that no-one liked to play — or watch, for the most part. 'Not pretty, but pretty effective' was how Charlton described his approach. But those who dismissed them as donkeys did so at their peril, as they had players of genuine quality in Paul McGrath, Steve Staunton, Ray Houghton, and John Aldridge.

Isolated for security reasons in Sardinia, the group was plagued by bad weather and bad football. England scored only two goals in topping the group with a win and two draws. Holland and Ireland tied for second place, also with only two goals each and three draws from as many matches. All three made it to the next round; but, despite their skilful line-up, the Dutch looked as abysmal as Maradona's Argentina.

Round Two

Cameroon vs Columbia

Argentina vs Brazil

Czechoslovakia vs Costa Rica

West Germany vs the Netherlands

Republic of Ireland vs Romania

Italy vs Uruguay

Yugoslavia vs Spain

England vs Belgium

ABOVE: The way we were: Australian World Cup Squad 1974.
BELOW: Jimmy McKay, whose goal against South Korea sealed Australia's place at West Germany '74.
Photos courtesy of the Australian National Archive

All Hail
The Holy Grail
And Jimmy McKay
Who did not fail. (Anon)

Action from the home leg of the final qualification games for West Germany '74, between Australia and South Korea.
Photos courtesy of the Australian National Archive

Australia plays Uruguay in a 'friendly' at the Sydney Cricket Ground, 27 April 1974. Late in the match, Australian striker Ray Baartz was hit with a karate chop to the neck by Uruguayan defender Luis Garisto and, as a result, missed the 1974 World Cup. Photos courtesy of the Australian National Archive

RIGHT: World Cup 1938. French captain Etienne Mattler (R) and Italian captain Giuseppe Meazza (L) toss the coin before the start of their quarter-final match. Photo: AAP

BELOW: World Cup 1938. Marseille, France. Semi-Final. Italy vs Brazil. Italy's Voici Piola bursts through Brazil's Machado (left) and Domingos during the match. Photo: Popperfoto

ABOVE: The most debated moment in World Cup history.
Geoff Hurst scores(?) for England in the 1966 final against West Germany. Photo: AAP

BELOW: Italian captain Giacinto Facchetti holds off Brazil's Jairzinho during the final in Mexico, 1970. Photo: AAP

Poetry in motion: Johan Cruyff.
Photo: AAP

The return of the grievous angel. Paolo Rossi, followed by Brazil's Junior, in action against Brazil, Spain 1982.
Photo: Popperfoto

Johan Neeskens scores in the final against West Germany, 1974. The Germans' first touch of the ball in the match was to retrieve it from the back of the net, but they went on to win.

Maradona vs England, quarter-final, Mexico 1986.
Photo AAP

Enter the Dragon. German captain Lothar Matthaus, France 1998.
Photo AAP

Ooh aah Paul McGrath.

French captain Zinedine Zidane heads home the first of his two goals against Brazil in the final of France. 1998.
Photo AAP

ABOVE: 'If I had been born ugly, you would never have heard of Pelé'.
George Best, the greatest player never to play in the World Cup finals.

RIGHT: Crowds line the streets as George Best's funeral cortege heads towards Parliament, at Stormont, in Belfast, Northern Ireland.
Photo AAP

The second round produced some extraordinary match-ups, especially between local rivals Argentina and Brazil, and West Germany and the Netherlands. Brazil dominated Argentina from the kick-off. They played them off the park but, even with Carecca up front, were unable to register it on the scoreboard, which could easily have read 6–0, especially as they managed to hit the wood-work three times. After eighty minutes of Brazilian dominance, a simple right-foot pass from Maradona to Canniggia produced the game's only goal and sent Brazil home. It was as if the football gods were punishing them for abandoning their sacred vocation of *jogo bonito*. Unlike 1982 and '86, when their departure from the tournament was met with genuine shock and sadness from all fans, this time they were not missed. Their anonymous brand of football ended in an undistinguished exit that went unnoticed.

West Germany and Holland put on a display that was every bit as nasty and mean-spirited as anything Uruguay had ever served up. The only difference was that this didn't seem to be a matter of team philosophy, but more a case of special individual efforts, in particular from Rijkaard and Voller, who were both sent off after twenty minutes. Jurgen Koehler was disgraceful, as usual. West Germany won the match, 2–1.

In Rome, Uruguay played well against Italy, but seemed unable or unwilling to chance their arm going forward; as a result Italy won 2–0, with Schillaci scoring again. Cameroon pipped Colombia 2–1 in extra time, thanks to two goals from the ageless Roger Milla and Colombian keeper Rene Higuita, who made an error 'as big as a house'. Czechoslovakia pumped tiny Costa Rica 4–1, with Skuhravy knocking in a hat-trick. Ireland and Romania fought out a tense, goalless arm-wrestle before the Irish went through on penalties. Yugoslavia beat Spain 2–1 in extra time, and England held off a determined Belgium 1–0, with Gascoigne creating a goal for David Platt in the final minute of extra time.

Argentina were playing like blue green algae — the worse they got, the further they went. They met Yugoslavia in the first quarter-final, which failed to produce a goal and so was eventually decided 3–2 in Argentina's favour in a penalty shoot-out. To cap off a dirty day, Maradona missed his penalty. Italy beat the heroic but unimaginative Ireland 1–0, which was a blow to lovers of romance and a great relief to lovers of football who were not from the Emerald Isle.

Having started the tournament in swashbuckling fashion, West Germany had reverted to type and to negative, over-cautious, and dull football. They ground out a professional 1–0 victory over Czechoslovakia, and were into the semi-finals. Cameroon, on the other hand, had taken swashbuckling action to levels not seen since the days of Blackbeard the pirate. Leading 2–1, with less than ten minutes to go in the quarter-final against England, the Indomitable Lions let their brutal tackling ruin what should have been their finest hour. First, they conceded a penalty just minutes before the final whistle, which Gary Lineker dutifully converted to send the match into extra time; and then, as if they couldn't help themselves, they gave away another penalty deep in extra time, to gift-wrap the victory for England. It was a wasted opportunity; but still, having made the quarter-finals, it was the best result ever for an African team at the World Cup. England marched on to the semi-finals, while Cameroon were left to ponder what might have been.

Italy met Argentina in the first semi-final, which was held in Maradona's adopted home town, Naples. Strangely, Italian coach Vicini dropped Baggio in favour of Vialli, despite the fact that he had developed a real understanding with the little Sardinian Schillaci over the course of the tournament. His judgement seemed vindicated though when, after seventeen minutes, Vialli created the opportunity for Schillaci, who scored his fifth goal for the tournament. With a 1–0 lead, the Italians retreated into themselves, unsure of whether to press for a conclusive goal or defend their narrow advantage. Argentina made the most of their opponent's uncertainty, and finally found their way into the game. Halfway through the second half they equalised through Caniggia, and at full-time they were still deadlocked at 1–1.

If there was an unwritten theme to Italy 1990 it was defensive, cynical, and sometimes spiteful play that resulted in a spate of yellow and red cards, and in too many matches being decided, begrudgingly, on penalties. This match was no exception, with six yellow cards and one red card being handed out; and with neither side willing to take their chances on creating a winning goal, the game went to a shoot-out. After six spot kicks each it was still all-square. Suddenly, Italy fell to pieces, missing their last two penalties and, unbelievably, handing a place in the final to Argentina.

West Germany faced England in the second semi-final in Turin, and the English turned on their best performance of the tournament. After a goalless first half, they were unlucky to concede a fluke goal to Andreas Brehme early in the second half. But, with ten minutes to go, Lineker once again came to England's rescue with a typically precise finish to equalise at 1–1 that sent the match to the apparently inevitable penalty shoot-out. If England had luck on their side in the quarter-final against Cameroon, it deserted them now. German goalkeeper Bodo Illgner emerged as the hero of the day, saving a shot from Stuart Pearce, and Chris Waddle became the villain, firing his penalty attempt over the crossbar. The final of Italy 1990 would be a re-match of the '86 final: Argentina vs Germany.

As the final match of Italy 1990 unfolded, it was almost impossible to look back on Cameroon's performance in the opening game, exactly one month ago in Milan, and realise that both matches were part of the same tournament. The final was an abomination — things started badly and quickly headed south.

Paying the price for their spate of fouls in the semi-final, Argentina was without Giusti, Canniggia, Olarticoechea, and Batista who were all suspended. Maradonna had a badly swollen ankle and looked fat, unfit, and bloated with self-pity. Germany played without creativity or adventure — as if, after winning the semi-final through a penalty shoot-out, they had discovered a successful formula and were intent on forcing a stalemate. The final also produced a couple of dubious firsts: the first players sent off in a World Cup final (Monzon and Dezotti from Argentina), and the first final to be decided by a penalty, which was professionally executed by Brehme five minutes before time.

Germany's triumph meant that it joined Italy and Brazil with three wins as the most successful team in World Cup history. It was also a great personal triumph for their coach, Franz Beckenbauer, who became the first man to win a World Cup as both captain and coach. Despite the historic significance, the tournament left a bad taste in the mouth of fans. Negative tactics, professional fouls, diving, low scores, and teams playing for penalty shoot-outs were making the beautiful game look ugly. Something had to be done — but what?

USA 1994

A bold new frontier … the beautiful game meets the beautiful people … Roberto Baggio: welcome to my nightmare

The fifteenth World Cup of football was announced in an atmosphere more reminiscent of Scott's race for the South Pole or Livingstone's search for the source of the Nile than anything that had previously accompanied a World Cup tournament. This was a real expedition to conquer uncharted territory. The prize? The last frontier: the USA and one hundred million television viewers just waiting to be converted to the beautiful game. With it came hundreds of millions of dollars in TV rights, merchandising, sponsorship, and the potential to develop professional domestic leagues. The United States stood beckoning to FIFA like the tales of Inca gold to Cortez.

The USA had been looming on football's horizon for a remarkably long time without the game ever really arriving. Many fans are surprised to learn that the United States contested the first World Cup ever in 1930, and had backed it up with appearances in 1934, 1950, and 1990. They had almost secured the right to host the 1986 tournament when Columbia were forced to withdraw, but lost out to Mexico right at the death. And, of course, there had been the North American Soccer League during the 1970s that had featured Pele, Franz Beckenbauer, Johann Cruyff, and George Best, not to mention Australia's own Adrian Alston. The league had flourished briefly, especially in New York (home of the

Cosmos) and Florida and California, thanks to their large Latin American populations, but faded once the marquee players retired. Then it collapsed in a heap, leaving behind the odd relic of yet another failed expedition into football's new world, rather like frozen climbers deserted on the slopes of Mount Everest.

Finally, in 1994, FIFA decided that now was the time, and a new and improved world game was taken to the shores of the USA. One hundred and forty nations competed for 24 spots at the finals — a new record. The often cynical displays by some teams at Italy '90 had left a bad taste in everyone's mouth; and so, recognising that the game was in trouble, FIFA decided it was time for a spring clean, and brought in some changes. Three points were awarded for a win, making it less desirable to slog it out for a draw; referees were instructed to crack down on time-wasting and tackling from behind; a new, high-tech ball that dipped and swerved alarmingly was introduced to make the goalkeeper's life even more hellish; and, finally, every player was made to sign a code of conduct that sought to reconnect with the spirit of the game.

The tournament began with the usual Hollywood hoop-la, climaxing with Diana Ross taking a penalty shot from about one metre out from goal and putting it wide — a portent of things to come. America is a land of contradictions, and the tournament was to be no exception. While the heart of the storm was pure, beautiful football and frenzied support, the vast majority of the USA's population remained oblivious to the fact that the greatest show on earth was even in town.

The qualifiers for USA '94 were grouped thus:

Group A	Group B
USA, Switzerland, Columbia, Romania	Cameroon, Brazil, Sweden, Russia

Group C	Group D
Germany, Spain, South Korea, Bolivia	Argentina, Bulgaria, Greece, Nigeria
Group E	Group F
Italy, Norway, Republic of Ireland, Mexico	Belgium, Holland, Saudi Arabia, Morocco

Pre-tournament favouritism was complicated. Brazil, as always, were mentioned in dispatches; however, their last campaign had been such a failure that a question marked remained, despite the presence of Romario, Bebeto, and Leonardo. Italy were very much in the frame, especially after their showing four years earlier, but coach Arrigo Sacchi had bet everything on one man, Roberto Baggio. A unified German team looked formidable, but had struggled to find a successful combination in front of goal. To this end, the ageing Rudi Voeller had been recalled to assist striker and captain Jurgen Klinsman.

Columbia were the surprise packet from South America. They had blitzed the qualification stage, even forcing the mighty Argentina into the undignified necessity of a play-off against Australia, which prompted the great Diego Maradona to come out of retirement. With Valderama in the midfield, the Columbians looked a more balanced and mature side than four years earlier. The best roughie was definitely Nigeria. People who were worth listening to had begun talking seriously about the possibility of an African nation winning the World Cup. Cameroon had all but made it to the semi-finals in Italy before shooting themselves in both feet simultaneously. If anything, Nigeria looked a stronger all-round team and, importantly, looked to have the necessary discipline and control.

Notable absentees were France, still reeling from the '82 and '86 campaigns, and England. The European champions from

1992, Denmark, were also missing, as were Yugoslavia, which was in the process of tearing itself apart in the Balkans War.

The tournament began under clear, blue skies and in blistering heat (so severe that it would effect match results), with title-holders Germany meeting minnows Bolivia. The Bolivians were making their first appearance back at the World Cup since 1950, when they had gone down in a cliffhanger to Uruguay 8–0. The Germans struggled against the heat and a resolute Bolivia before Klinsman finally beat the offside trap, fifteen minutes into the second half, to score. In response, the Bolivians sent on their best player, injured striker Marco Etchervery, who proceeded to get himself sent off within four minutes. The final score was 1–0 to Germany.

Other matches in Group C included a thrilling 2–2 draw between Spain and South Korea. Spain led 2–0 going into the last five minutes of the game before the industrious Koreans clawed their way back into the game, eventually getting the equaliser in injury time. Germany and Spain played out a 1–1 draw that said nothing about either side, while Bolivia and Korea also drew 0–0. Spain then drilled Bolivia 3–1, but needed a penalty from a blatant dive to lock-in its place in round two, while Germany got home 3–2 against a marvellously spirited South Korean side who had simply hit their stride too late. One unexpected upshot of the German victory was defender Stefan Effenberg being sent home for making a rude gesture at his own fans, who happened to be abusing him at the time. Ah, those whacky, zany Germans. Spain and Germany went through to round two.

In Group A, the hosts, USA, had to deal not only with their own expectations but also the pressing needs of the tournament. It was the general consensus that, for USA '94 to succeed, the hosts had to make it at least as far as round two. Their first match, against a highly organised Switzerland, featuring Chapuisat and Sutter, ended in a respectable 1–1 draw. Already we were starting to see the effect of the new ball, which dipped and swerved so mania-cally that it made shots from a distance and especially free kicks a real threat. Both goals in the USA vs Switzerland game came from free kicks. In the first big shock, Gheorghe Hagi's Romania carved up the highly fancied Columbians 3–1. Hagi had a hand in all the Romanian goals, but his own solo effort, an audacious, inch-perfect chip from the left touch-line, about twenty-five metres out, was an early candidate for goal of the tournament.

With Raducioiu and Petrescu in their posse, the Romanians looked mighty fine — that is, until four days later when the highly organised Swiss drilled more holes in them than a tasty Emmental, thumping Romania 4–1. This made the balance of power very interesting, and the USA now met Columbia in a game that could decide the group. The game was a tense arm-wrestle until Columbian defender Andres Escobar lunged to intercept a pass and accidentally put it into the back of his own net to give the USA a 1–0 advantage. Both sides scored again, but ultimately Escobar's own-goal was to be the difference between the two teams, with USA winning 2–1. Shock waves went through the football world. Despite winning their final group game against Switzerland, Columbia were the only team eliminated from their group and were on their way home.

Later it emerged that the Columbian coach and particular team members had received death threats from Columbian cartels, warning them of the consequences of failure at the World Cup. A few days after returning home to Medellin in Columbia, Andres Escobar was murdered outside a nightclub. According to his girl-friend, the killer shouted 'goal' each time he shot Escobar. FIFA briefly considered abandoning the tournament, but decided that the show must go on.

Group B kicked off with a pulsating 2–2 draw between Sweden and a strangely inhibited Cameroon. The spirit of the

Lions was being eaten away by squabbles about pay and conditions, and it showed in their play. Brazil defeated Russia 2–0 with consummate ease and then carved up the lacklustre Cameroon, 3–0. Business as usual. Sweden beat Russia 3–1 with Dahlin, Brolin, and Andersson starring for the Swedes, and it was looking like game, set, and match for Group B.

But the action was just starting. Russia faced the now totally dispirited Cameroon in a dead rubber and beat them 6–1, with Oleg Salenko scoring a World Cup-record five goals for the match. In the final group game, Sweden shocked everyone by coming out and attacking Brazil and forcing them into defending. The Brazilians suddenly looked poor, and Sweden took an early lead through a goal by Andersson. But with a one-goal advantage, the Swedes sat back to defend their lead and so allowed the Brazilians back into the game. Romario equalised and both sides settled for the 1–1 draw. Brazil and Sweden went through to the next round; Oleg Salenko went back to Russia, where he is now a successful shoe salesman.

Group D got underway with the now born-again Maradona's Argentina slaughtering debutants Greece 4–0. With striker Batistuta on fire and completing a hat-trick, it could easily have been 10–0. Just like the Soviets in 1986, Argentina had intimidated everyone with the strength of their opening performance. Nigeria took a page out of their book and smashed Bulgaria 3–0, and you didn't have to be Einstein to figure out where this group was heading.

Four days later, Maradona spearheaded Argentina to a 2–1 win over Nigeria. It was a terrific match, and the telecast ended with shots of a smiling Maradona being led off for a routine drug test. Meanwhile, Bulgaria, led by Hristo Stoichkov, bounced back from their opening loss to crush Greece 4–0, and suddenly the group was alive again. Nigeria kept this very tight group on a knife-edge when they beat the hapless Greeks (who by now looked as though they just wished the whole miserable business was over) 2–0, to set up a must-win clash in the final group game between Argentina and Bulgaria.

But the make-or break match was overshadowed by the news that Maradona had tested positive to illegal stimulants and, in the biggest doping scandal since Ben Johnson, was out of the tournament. Maradona protested his innocence and, while no-one will ever know the truth about the counter-allegations that went back and forth, all that mattered was that the heart had been torn out of the most convincing team in the tournament. With all this in the background, Bulgaria came out and stole the match 2–0, to qualify second after Nigeria, with the now shell-shocked Argentines going through as one of the best third place-getters.

If this wasn't high drama enough, Group E began with another huge upset. In front of a massive crowd at Giants Stadium, Jack Charlton's fighting Irish landed a magnificent uppercut to KO the blue-blood Italians, 1–0, courtesy of a Ray Houghton stunner. The match was a thriller, and took on historic significance as it was played out in front of the very large Irish and Italian expatriate and immigrant communities living around New York.

Norway then managed to beat Mexico 1–0 in another upset before facing up to an Italian side that knew it had its whole tournament to play for. On paper, the Italians were a much better team, but Norway were playing above themselves and the *Azzurri* were hampered by injury. Italy started the match looking second rate; then, to complicate matters, Gianluca Pagliuca was sent off after twenty minutes. It was a disaster. Unbelievably, Italian coach Sacchi reacted by immediately taking off star striker Roberto Baggio. Somehow the Italians dug in and gradually turned the game's momentum their way, eventually getting the vital victory 1–0 to vindicate the coach's decision.

Mexico beat Ireland 2–1 in blistering heat, in a match made memorable when Irish coach Jack Charlton was banned from the touchline after arguing with the FIFA official who had refused to allow an Irish substitution for several minutes. The group ended in a neat symmetry, when in the final matches Italy drew with Mexico 1–1 and Ireland and Norway drew 0–0. So all four teams finished on four points, with goal difference deciding who progressed to the next round. Mexico, Ireland, and Italy qualified while Norway went home.

The final group got underway with Belgium defeating more fancied Morocco 1–0 while their neighbours, Holland, struggled to defeat Saudi Arabia 2–1. The Dutch looked good, but were missing their best players, Van Basten and Gullit — a big minus in any language. Clashes between local rivals always produce something special, and this was certainly the case next match when Holland and Belgium met in the battle of the Benelux. Belgium sensationally defeated their star-studded rivals 1–0, with Belgian goalkeeper Prudhomme voted man of the match in one of the finest goalkeeping performances that I have ever seen. When Saudi Arabia defeated Morocco 2–1 on the same day, it ensured that Group F was going to be as tight as the others and also threatened the possibility of another shock elimination.

In the final two group games, Holland accounted for Morocco 2–1, but not before suffering a mild coronary, and Saudi Arabia defeated Belgium 1–0, with Said Owarian scoring one of the great individual goals in World Cup history, to secure their place in round two. With the first three teams all finishing equal on six points, only Morocco was heading home.

The first round had produced a death, a drug scandal, a lot of red cards, a return to attacking football and, most importantly, more drama than *Gone With the Wind*. The draw for the round of sixteen looked like this:

Round Two

Spain vs Switzerland

Belgium vs Germany

Saudi Arabia vs Sweden

Romania vs Argentina

Brazil vs USA

Holland vs Ireland

Nigeria vs Italy

Mexico vs Bulgaria

The only real shock elimination, so far, had been Colombia. The tournament was looking wide open.

The second round of matches began with Spain unexpectedly dominating Switzerland 3–0. The new 'interpretative' offside rule, based on the concept of a player being 'passively' offside, caused confusion within the Swiss defence and cost them dearly. Belgium met Germany in a one-sided match that was affected by the Belgians' interrupted preparation — they had only had two days to prepare, and problems with flights and accommodation, while the Germans had a four-day break and were playing in Chicago, where their group games had been based. Germany won 3–2, but the result was almost over-shadowed by the referee refusing to award a clear-cut penalty to the Belgians that cost them the chance to equalise. The referee would later admit his error and apologise, but the damage had been done.

In forty-degree heat in Dallas, Sweden flexed their collective muscles and kicked sand in the face of their Saudi opponents with an emphatic 3–1 victory. Dahlin and Andersson again did the damage; with keeper Ravelli in outstanding form, they were beginning to attract some real attention. In the best game of the tournament so far, Gheorghe Hagi's Romania eliminated the now Maradona-less Argentina 3–2 with a magnificent display of attacking football. The devil-may-care Romanians were through to the quarter-finals, and the most impressive team from the first round was on its way home.

In a fourth of July extravaganza, the USA lost to Brazil, in a controversial and sometimes ill-tempered affair, 1–0. Brazil seemed to be getting worse with each game and looked more vulnerable the further the tournament progressed. It was very unusual, but they were still alive, and no-one in their right mind would bet against them. The Dutch defeated the Irish on the back of a howler from Irish keeper Pat Bonner, and with their elimination ended a golden era which had a significance in Ireland beyond mere football.

The match of the round looked to be Nigeria vs Italy, and it didn't disappoint. With the Nigerians leading 1–0 late in the second half, Gianfranco Zola was sensationally sent off for … nothing. Replays showed clearly that he had made no contact at all with the Nigerian defender, but the damage was done. One goal and one man down, the Italians looked lost until Roberto Baggio arrived like the cavalry to rescue Sacchi's Italy with a last-minute equaliser. A second goal to Baggio, courtesy of a penalty in extra time, was enough to eliminate the impressive Nigerians. Sitting on a 1–0 lead, they had reverted to a European style by trying to close down the game, and it had cost them a place in the quarter-finals.

In the last game of the second round, Bulgaria defeated America's second team, Mexico, on penalties after an entertaining 1–1 draw. So, the quarter-final matches would be:

Quarter Finals	
Italy vs Spain	Holland vs Brazil
Romania vs Sweden	Bulgaria vs Germany

Italy and Spain produced as nasty a contest as the new rules would allow. Ultimately, the Italians overcame a very gallant Spain 2–1, but again only made it with minutes to spare. Both Baggios scored, and the *Azzurri* were starting to look like contenders. Holland and Brazil met the same day, and turned on another classic in the archive of great World Cup games. Tactically the match was a real gem; unfortunately, Brazil's winning goals came out of confusion over the new, passive offside rule. Twice the Dutch defenders stopped when Brazilians looked to be offside, twice the flag stayed down, and twice the Brazilians scored. In the end, Brazil won 3–2 to show the doubters they were back in town.

Bulgaria were going into unknown territory; in fact, before this tournament they had never won a World Cup match. But that was before the arrival of Hristo Stoichkov. He looked a bit like the human equivalent of the chicken hawk from the Foghorn Leghorn cartoon: all 'piss and vinegar' with an ego the size of Mt Rushmore, but also the ability to back it up. He could often be seen giving opponents and referees an explosive burst of profanities in Bulgarian — they didn't know what he was saying but, somehow, everyone got the message. If they were to continue their unprecedented success at the tournament, they would now need to achieve another 'first' and defeat Germany.

As the quarter-final got underway, the Germans looked to have things under control. Early in the first half they took the lead through a Lothar Matthaus goal, and seemed to have the match won. But, gradually, the tide began to turn, and the Bulgarians found their way back into the game. Fifteen minutes before full-time they won a free kick, and Stoichkov strode up like Clint Eastwood in a spaghetti Western and nonchalantly nailed the free kick to equalise for Bulgaria. Momentum was now running with them, and minutes later Letchov scored to give the Bulgarians a memorable victory.

It was *auf wiedersehen* Germany, their earliest exit from the World Cup since 1962. Jurgen Klinsman left the field in tears.

The last quarter-final also featured an eastern European side with a mercurial leader up against one of the big boys from the west, when Hagi's Romania took on Sweden in San Francisco. After a mighty struggle that went into extra time and ended 2–2 with two goals to Raducioiu, Romania were eliminated yet again on penalties.

The first semi-final between Italy and Bulgaria at Giants Stadium was a tough and absorbing struggle between two in-form teams. It also featured the tournament's leading goal scorer, Stoichkov, but it was Italian striker Baggio who took the initiative with an absolute wonder goal in the twentieth minute. He followed this almost immediately with a second, more run-of-the-mill but no less valuable effort five minutes later. Stoichkov managed to get one back for Bulgaria in the dying minutes of the first half, but Italy looked to have the game under control.

With Italy cruising to victory in the second half, a combination of bad luck and bad management threw their plans for the final into jeopardy. Coach Sacchi decided to leave his stars on the field to play out the match, and the move backfired when Baggio tore a hamstring. Surely, he was now out of the final. Then Alessandro Costacurta picked up a second yellow card, which meant that he, too, would join the list of suspended or injured Italians not available for selection in the final.

The other semi-final between Sweden and Brazil promised a reprise of the close-fought draw between the two sides from round one, when Sweden had pressured the South Americans onto the back foot with attacking football. However, they looked like two entirely different teams when they took the field in Los Angeles, and the match turned out to be the greatest anti-climax since the invention of the chastity belt.

Sweden couldn't manage a single shot on goal, not so much through Brazilian pressure as their own timid approach to the game. It was as if, in the semi-final of the World Cup, they didn't dare to win the game out of fear of losing it. To make matters worse, Brazil saved their worst performance of the entire tournament for the semi. They looked utterly beatable but, luckily for them, Sweden didn't even try. In the end Brazil got the result, through a goal from Romario ten minutes from full-time, and Sweden went out, to their ultimate disgrace, without so much as a whimper.

Despite all the twists and turns of the tournament, and the heroics of Stoichkov, Hagi, and Salenko, the final delivered the two teams most pundits had predicted from the start: Italy and Brazil. The South Americans would be virtually at full strength, while the *Azzurri* were ravaged by injury and suspension. Baggio played despite injury with his thigh heavily strapped, and 34-year-old Baresi came into the starting line-up for the first time since round one.

Brazil defended much better than the Italians and looked to be in control, but again Romario and Bebeto had left their scoring boots at home and they weren't able to register their side's superiority on the scoreboard. Baggio was very clearly hampered by injury and was effectively a passenger for the entire, excruciating match.

The tournament had been full of innovations, and the final produced another original moment when it meandered to a goal-less draw after extra-time. For the first time in World Cup history the final would be decided on penalties. Today, everyone remembers that Roberto Baggio missed his spot-kick and that Italy lost; what they forget is that, before him, Baresi and Massaro for Italy and Santos for Brazil also missed penalties. But history is cruel.

Regardless of Baggio's agony and the manner of the victory, Brazil had won the World Cup trophy for an unprecedented fourth time and had finally managed to successfully marry the dazzling attacking skills traditionally associated with *jogo bonito* with the more disciplined, pragmatic approach to defence favoured by European teams. After two previous failed attempts in 1974 and 1990, their willingness to persevere showed how much they had learned from the lessons of the past — most notably 1950, 1954, and 1966. Football purists might be dismayed by the route they had taken, but could not argue with the result. Efficiency or exuberance? This is always a tough choice, particularly if you are Brazilian.

France 1998

Romanian blondes have more fun … Suker's surprise … Ronaldo seizures the day but Z Z's tops

In 1998 the sixteenth World Cup of football returned to the home of its founder, Jules Rimet. Seventy years earlier, the Frenchman's vision of a world championship of football had taken root and had grown steadily to become the biggest sporting event in the world. On its return to France it was bigger and brighter than ever. There was a new sheriff in town: Sepp Blatter was the new FIFA president, and his first innovation was to increase the number of teams at France '98 from twenty-four to thirty-two, making it a truly cosmopolitan celebration of world football.

His second initiative was to try to eliminate the tackle from behind. Whereas it had previously been frowned upon, Blatter declared war on it and directed referees to give a red card to any player performing this dangerous and dubious skill. It was a move that met with near universal applause.

The largest-ever group of World Cup qualifiers were:

Group A
Brazil, Morocco,
Scotland, Norway

Group B
Italy, Cameroon,
Chile, Austria

Group C
France, Saudi Arabia,
Denmark, South Africa

Group D
Paraguay, Spain,
Nigeria, Bulgaria

Group E
South Korea, Holland,
Belgium, Mexico

Group F
Yugoslavia, Iran,
Germany, USA

Group G
England, Romania,
Colombia, Tunisia

Group H
Argentina, Japan,
Croatia, Jamaica

There were new faces, in debutants Croatia, South Africa, Jamaica, and Japan, but pre-tournament favouritism settled on the old and familiar Brazil. Aside from the fact that they would probably start favourites even if they failed to qualify, they were defending champions with notable additions to the team in Ronaldo, Rivaldo, and Denilson to complement the experience of Bebeto and Roberto Carlos. Germany were also in the mix, but looked to be an unbalanced side. However, in striker Oliver Bierhof, they had a classic 1950s–1960s-style centre-forward, who, given the right supply, could become another Gerd Muller.

The hosts, France, had a good squad with one truly remarkable player — midfield genius Zinedine Zidane. The questions for them were in front of goal. Italy, with the del Piero–Vieri–Baggio combination, looked great on paper, but could coach Cesare Maldini (yes, folks, the man who lent his name to 'Maldini Moments') get it to work on the field? The skilful Holland had been pretty unlucky at USA '94 and, under the direction of Guus Hiddink, looked to have gone up a notch since then. Argentina also looked good, but the age-old question about South Americans in Europe lingered in many people's minds. Finally, England were also rated a genuine chance this time. In Alan Shearer they had a goal poacher of the highest quality and he was backed up by a speedy, young kid called Michael Owen who looked like he could give the English something they had lacked since the War of the Roses: unpredictability.

The opening match of Group A saw champions Brazil take on poor wee Scotland, who were still looking to break their duck and progress past the first round of the tournament. The Scots were right in it at half-time, with the scores locked at 1–1, until an unlucky own goal by Tom Boyd sealed victory for Brazil and added another unhappy chapter to the saga of the tartan experience. Morocco and Norway settled for a 2–2 draw, after an exciting match in which Moroccan midfielder Hadji had scored a fabulous goal to give his side an early lead. Six days later, Norway and Scotland played out another draw, 1–1, the highlight being a textbook 'Route 1' goal by Scotland and Celtic's Craig Burley (it's really worth a look if you get the chance). Next up, Brazil showed all that they would take some beating for the title when they put Morocco to the sword 3–0, with Ronaldo, Rivaldo, and Bebeto all getting on the score sheet.

So far, Group A had followed the script; now we started to see some improvisation. Going into the final group games, both Morocco and Scotland fancied their chances to progress through to the next round along with Brazil, after the Brazilians inevitably beat Norway. Not so fast, boys. The Brazil vs Norway game provided the first real upset of the tournament when Norway came back from 1–0 down — first to level the scores with just seven minutes left in the match, and then to win the game, 2–1, in the last minute of play. The result came as a shock to everyone, but perhaps it shouldn't have. If you recall the trouble the Swedes had given Brazil in USA '94, maybe there is something in the Scandinavian style of play that upsets the Brazilian's rhythm.

Meanwhile, Morocco, believing they were playing for a future in the tournament, smashed a ten-man Scotland, 3–0. The sight of the Moroccans celebrating their place in the second round only to hear that Norway had done the unthinkable remains the most poignant moment from the 1998 World Cup. Laughter turned to tears as one of the bright lights of the tournament realised they were going home — *c'est la guerre*.

Group B began with a turgid affair between Austria and Cameroon that ended in a 1–1 draw. A forgettable match was made memorable by two highlights: Cameroon's goal, a piece of individual brilliance from Pierre Njanka who, after eighty minutes of frustration, was mad as hell and not going to take it any more, and Austria's equaliser late in injury time. Italy vs Chile produced a fascinating struggle between two class teams: Chile, led by Zamorano and Salas, and Italy, spearheaded by Vieri and Baggio. But it was as much a game for psychology buffs as football fans. With Chile leading 2–1 late in the game, Italy were awarded a crucial penalty. Without hesitation, Roberto Baggio stepped forward to take it. After the final of USA '94, the enormity of the moment was not lost on anyone. Badabing, 2–2, and redemption.

Chile and Austria then drew 1–1, with the Austrians scoring late in injury time and Italy carved up Cameroon 3–0, with Vieri and Luigi Di Biagio (two names that would ultimately be remembered for very different reasons) doing the damage. Italy were through to the second round, but who would join them? With everything to play for, Austria succumbed, 2–1, to Italy with Vieri and Baggio scoring again. Austria managed their only goal (you guessed it) late in injury time, for the third time in three outings. Oh, well. I guess it gave them something to talk about on the long drive home.

Meanwhile, Chile and Cameroon drew 1–1, with Cameroon equalising after being reduced to ten men when Rigobert Song, who seemed utterly determined to get himself sent off, finally succeeded. Sadly, Cameroon then scored a winning goal that was disallowed for no apparent reason, denying them a historic victory. Chile were through to round two despite not winning a game.

The big question dominating Group C was how far France could go playing without a striker. In their first match they fluked three goals against South Africa, to win 3–0. Next up, they were fortunate to knock in four goals against Saudi Arabia before completing the group stage with two lucky goals against Denmark, to qualify with maximum points and a goal difference of nine to one. How lucky can you get!

The race for second place in the group was very tight. Denmark began with a 1–0 win over Saudi Arabia, but impressed nobody with their ageing squad based around the Laudrup brothers and Manchester United's Peter Schmeichel. Next they met South Africa on a day that would ultimately become known as red card day. It seemed that Sepp Blatter was not happy with the enforcement of his edict on tackling from behind, and sent a very clear message to the referees that he wasn't joking. The result was that they handed out three red cards and seven yellows — the players took more free kicks than the Karate Kid. Benny McCarthy scored South Africa's first-ever World Cup goal, but Brian Laudrup got the Danes a share of the points and one foot in the next round. In the other game, France and Saudi Arabia got one red card each to make 18 June a day to remember.

South Africa and Saudi Arabia then sealed their own fates when they drew 2–2 in a match in which three penalties were awarded. Denmark joined France in the second round.

In Group D, Paraguay, led by the remarkable figure of Jose Luis Chilavert, began with a paralysingly dull 0–0 draw with a Bulgarian team which, unfortunately, bore no resemblance to the dynamic team from 1994, other than the fact that all the same players were in it. Nigeria twice came from behind to upset Spain 3–2. Sunday Oliseh scored a beauty for Nigeria, and Spanish keeper and captain Zubizaretta managed the howler of the tournament, a mistake that would cost Spain dearly.

By the time Nigeria met Bulgaria, two trends had become obvious. Shirt pulling had replaced hacking as the new blight on the game; but on the positive side, dramatic, late goals were all the rage. It seemed as though every other goal was scored in injury time, as if strikers around the world had been watching Alfred Hitchcock movies and had decided to add an element of suspense to their game.

Nigeria overcame a Bulgarian side who looked as though rigor mortis had set in, 1–0, and once again the final group games would be crucial in deciding who went on and who went home. With Okocha and Amokachi, Nigeria looked ready to rumble, as did Spain. On the other hand, Paraguay had managed two nil-all draws and looked as though they would struggle to score at a hen's night. But in giant upset number two, Paraguay put three goals past the Nigerians while Spain gave it to Bulgaria 6–1. Commentators observed that Bulgaria appeared to have stopped trying in the second half. How could you tell?, I wondered. But even six goals wasn't enough to save Spain, as they were overtaken by Paraguay, who joined Nigeria in round two.

Neighbours Holland and Belgium kicked off Group E with a tame 0–0 draw that did a lot more for the Belgians than it did for the Dutch. Sensing this, perhaps, an angry Holland took out their frustrations on Korea to the tune of 5–0. The score sheet read: Cocu, Bergkamp, Jonk, Overmars, and Davids. Add to that Kluivert, and you had six reasons why people thought the Dutch could go all the way. Maybe the Koreans had got a sense that it wasn't going to be their tournament when, prior to this thrashing, they let slip a 1–0 lead to lose to Mexico 3–1. As if wasting leads was catching, Belgium threw away a two-goal advantage to draw 2–2 with Mexico. It cost them a place in the next round. The group ended in draws all round when Korea held Belgium 1–1, and the masters of suspense, Mexico, scored once with barely fifteen minutes to go and then again in extra time to draw 2–2 with Holland.

In Group F, Germany and Yugoslavia were expected to qualify and they both managed it without too much trouble. The first round of group games was pretty straightforward, with the Germans accounting for USA 2–0 and Yugoslavia beating Iran 1–0. On 21 June Iran played USA in a historic encounter that ultimately provided a wonderful advertisement for sport over politics. Despite the tense background to the match, both teams embraced before the kick-off and then played the game in the right spirit, with Iran getting home 2–1 to the delight of their fans. It was the only victory for an Asian team at the tournament.

In the marquee match of the group, Yugoslavia led Germany 2–0 with goals to Stankovic and Stojkovic, before being run down 2–2. In the final group games, Iran held out until the second half before succumbing to Germany's dynamic forward duo of Bierhof and Klinsmann, 2–0, and Yugoslavia did enough to beat the USA, 1–0.

At a glance, Group G looked to be a possible group of death candidate, but all depended on Columbia. After the events of USA '94, it was amazing that they showed up at all; but, led by Carlos

Valderama (who looked like a perfect cross between Jimi Hendrix and Mitch Mitchell), they had the ability to cause some damage.

They went down in their first match against Romania, courtesy of a goal by Ilie in injury time in the first half. On the same day England got their campaign off to the right start with a comfortable 2–0 win over Tunisia. Next up, the Tunisians also went down to Columbia, but even in victory the Columbians looked a pale imitation of the team of '90 and '94. Still, the courage they had shown in participating negated any possible criticism of their performance.

In massive upset number three, Romania knocked off England 2–1, scoring first after seventy seconds and then getting the winner late in injury time after Michael Owen had scored to equalise with less than ten minutes left in the match. Romania were through to round two and England joined them when, in the final game, they scored twice inside half an hour to beat Columbia 2–0. In a colourful finale, the entire Romanian team took the field with matching bleached blonde hair for their final group game against Tunisia. It didn't help them much and they drew 1–1, but they certainly underlined themselves as a team to watch.

The final group began with a real curiosity when a pair of World Cup debutants in Jamaica and Croatia faced off. The Croats looked to have a really strong side with Suker, Boban, and Prosinecki, and first impressions reinforced this when they beat Jamaica 2–0 and then followed up with another victory against Japan. All you can do is beat the opposition you are given, and Croatia had done this to earn themselves a place in the second round. But were they any good? Maybe; maybe not.

Argentina beat Japan in a coma, then woke up to thrash Jamaica 5–0 with a double to Ortega and a hat-trick to Batistuta. Their final group match against Croatia would go a long way to answering questions about both sides. Or would it? As both teams had already qualified, there was a definite hint of Croatia taking it easy; nonetheless, Argentina won 1–0.

It had taken seventeen days but, finally, here we were at the knockout stage of the tournament. Surprise packets to have made it this far were Norway, Denmark, Paraguay, and the 'blondes have more fun' Romanians. Matches in the elimination phase saw the introduction of the 'golden goal' rule — in the event of a draw and extra time, whoever scored first won the game. Tally-ho. The final round of sixteen looked like this:

Round Two

Brazil vs Chile	Italy vs Norway
Nigeria vs Denmark	France vs Paraguay
Germany vs Mexico	Holland vs Yugoslavia
Argentina vs England	Romania vs Croatia

Brazil began with their most convincing display to date, a 4–1 thrashing of Chile, with doubles to Ronaldo and Cesar Sampaio. Chile had looked impressive and were probably unlucky to face such a stern test so early on. Italy did a professional 'meet and defeat' job on Norway, who had surprised even themselves by getting this far. The score was that old Italian favourite, 1–0, and the scorer a new Italian favourite, Christian Vieri.

But Denmark continued to fly the flag for Scandinavia, and upset the Nigerian Super Eagles 4–1. The apparently ageless Laudrup brothers (actually, they were thirty-four and twenty-nine respectively) had a romp, and suddenly the rest of the team was starting to look uncannily like the great Danes of 1986. After a titanic struggle, Laurent Blanc scored the first-ever golden goal to put France through and eliminate Paraguay. After the match, inspirational Paraguayan captain Chilavert provided the world with a quote that should be printed on every football, shirt, and pair of boots. When asked about the pressure of a World Cup elimination match he replied that there was no pressure, as this was just a football match. Real pressure, he said, was not knowing how you would feed your children — something Paraguayans face every day.

Germany predictably defeated Mexico, 2–1, with goals again coming from Bierhof and Klinsmann. Holland and Yugoslavia turned on the best match of the round so far, with a game that was both brilliant and nasty by turns and ever so dramatic. With the scores locked at 1–1, Yugoslav genius Predrag Mijatovic fired his penalty shot into the crossbar, only to see Edgar Davids score to give Holland victory in the final minute of play.

There was still more drama when England met old rival Argentina. Argentina took an early lead via a penalty after five minutes, but England drew level through the same method four minutes later. Michael Owen then put his side in front with a classic solo effort, only to see Zanetti equalise from a free kick one minute before half-time. And that was just the first half. Two minutes after the restart, David Beckham was sent off for nothing much, and it looked to be all over for England. But the English hung on; in fact, they did better than that, and when Sol Campbell scored with a header, one of the great victories of all time looked to be on the cards. As if the game needed another twist, the referee disallowed the goal, despite the replay proving inconclusive, and so the game finally was decided on penalties. Argentina won to reinforce their status as England's nemesis, and again the English were on their way home to think of what might have been.

In the final game of the round of sixteen, Davor Suker led Croatia to victory over a plucky Romania, 1–0, and the quarter-finalists of France '98 were settled:

┌──┐
│ **Quarter Finals** │
│ Italy vs France   Denmark vs Brazil │
│ Germany vs Croatia   Holland vs Argentina │
└──┘

The first quarter-final between Italy and France promised plenty, and delivered an enthralling tactical battle between the two European heavyweights. Half chances came and went for both sides; but neither team could manage to score, even after extra time, and so the game was decided on penalties. In a triumph of positive thinking, Baggio stepped up first for Italy and proved beyond any doubt that he had slain his demons when he scored. Unfortunately, his example wasn't followed by Albertini and di Biaggio, and once again Italy had failed in a penalty shoot-out at the World Cup.

Brazil and Denmark met in a new interpretation of David and Goliath, and turned on a cracker. Jorgensen put the Danes ahead after only two minutes and, after a see-sawing battle, Brazil were leading 3–2 in the final minute of play when Danish defender Rieper hit the crossbar with a looping header that would have taken the game to extra time.

If any of the quarter-finalists could have been accused of having an easy run so far it was Croatia, and questions still lingered about their ability against quality opposition. They put any doubts firmly to rest when, in their best performance of the tournament, they destroyed Germany, 3–0. German defender Worns was sent off five minutes before half-time, and from then on it was all Croatia. The goals were shared between and Jarni, Vlaovic, and the irrepressible Suker.

In the match for the final place in the semi-finals, Holland met Argentina at the Velodrome in Marseille. In a game of elegant symmetry, both teams got a goal (Holland through Kluivert and

Argentina through Lopez) and a red card (to Dutchman Numan and Argentine Ortega) and the game seemed to have extra time written all over it when, in the last minute of normal time, a piece of sheer magic from Denis Bergkamp sent the Netherlands through, 2–1.

The semi-final pairings were intriguing; for once, any of the four teams would be worthy finalists. Brazil and Holland produced a great game in which neither side could do more than hold their own. After an even first half, Ronaldo gave Brazil the lead in the first minute of the second half, but then the Dutchmen really took the game up to them and deservedly equalised through Kluivert to send the game to extra time. Neither side could find a 'golden goal' and so everything came down to the dreaded penalty shoot-out. History shows that the Dutch lost in the shoot-out; it was through no fault of their own but, rather, thanks to two magnificent saves from Brazilian keeper Claudio Taffarel.

In an equally dramatic second semi-final, France defeated Croatia 2–1, courtesy of two second-half goals from Lilian Thuram — the only goals he ever scored for his country. In a minor scuffle, Slaven Bilic won an Academy Award nomination for himself and a red card for Laurent Blanc, which would cost the French captain a place in the World Cup final. Croatia went on to win the play-off for third place to finally silence their detractors and complete the fairy-tale debut.

So the final produced a classic confrontation: the tournament hosts against the reigning champions. On the morning of the match, star Brazilian forward Ronaldo suffered what was described as a stress-related fit. Panic swept through Brazil's hotel, with players being woken by cries of 'he's dead, he's dead'. The striker had apparently swallowed his tongue during the convulsions; although it left him with few physical effects, it was clear that he was badly shaken by what had happened.

In a bizarre footnote, team management tried to cover up what had happened and then promptly announced their team for the final, minus the world's best striker. Fifteen minutes later, he was, miraculously, back in the side. Normally, when the Brazilians left for their matches there was a party atmosphere with singing and music, but the whole affair had seriously unsettled the team and they travelled to the game in silence. Ronaldo took the field but made little impression on the game.

The French came out with all guns blazing, and Zinedine Zidane emphatically stamped his credentials as a champion when he seized the game by the scruff of the neck with two first-half goals. Emmanuel Petit put the result beyond doubt with a third goal late in the second half and, in keeping with the pattern of the tournament, Marcel Desailly got himself sent off. France had won the World Cup in France — *allez les bleues*.

Korea/Japan 2002

Into the Rising Sun ... Hup Hiddink! ... the twilight of the gods — sayonara Monsieur Zidane

The seventeenth World Cup was held outside of Europe and the Americas for the first time. It also marked the first time that the tournament had been co-hosted. One hundred and ninety-eight teams entered before being reduced to a final twenty-nine to join defending champions France and co-hosts Korea and Japan. Along with the usual suspects, debutants Senegal, Ecuador, China, and Slovenia made it to the party. In keeping with the feeling of true internationalism marked by the journey into Asia, Korea/Japan 2002 would be the first time that teams from Europe, North and South America, Africa, and Asia would all make the quarter-finals of the tournament.

Pre-tournament favouritism was a predictable affair, centred around five teams. Argentina and you-know-who were the pick from South America, the former on account of their irresistible form in qualifying, and the latter because they were there. Based on their form at Euro 2000, title-holders France and Portugal were seen as not having a struck match between them, with Italy a slightly less popular bet among pundits but still a strong favourite.

The groups for Korea/ Japan were:

Group A
France, Senegal,
Denmark, Uruguay

Group B
Spain, Paraguay,
South Africa, Slovenia

Group C
Brazil, Turkey,
China, Costa Rica,

Group D
South Korea, Poland,
USA, Portugal

Group E
Republic of Ireland, Germany,
Cameroon, Saudi Arabia

Group F
England, Sweden,
Argentina, Nigeria

Group G
Croatia, Italy,
Mexico, Ecuador.

Group H
Japan, Belgium,
Russia, Tunisia

The tournament began on 31 May with one of the greatest upsets in World Cup history when France met and were beaten by first-timers Senegal, 1–0. The Senagalese, led by El Hadj Diouf, ripped into their former colonial masters, who were without the injured Zinedine Zidane. The French appeared strangely lack-lustre, but, still, the result was up there with Cameroon's victory over Argentina in 1990. The following day Denmark easily accounted for a disappointing Uruguay, 2–1. Perversely, Uruguay had opted to play Sebastian Abreu up-front ahead of Diego Forlan, a proven performer in top European competition.

The Zidaneless France then met Uruguay five days later with the match ending in a 0–0 draw. Denmark obliged everyone by playing out a 1–1 draw with Senegal, thereby setting up a thrilling finish in which any of the four teams could go through to the next round, depending on the results of the last group games. Alarm bells were ringing for the French. Rumours were circulating about their players not attending training and being seen in casinos the night before matches, but most worrying of all was the simple fact that in one hundred and twenty minutes of football they had failed to score a goal.

With everything to play for, Denmark, led by Rommedahl, Sand, and Jon Dahl Tomasson defeated France 2–0 to complete a truly miserable tournament for les Bleues. The defending champion was going home, without a win, and without so much as troubling the scorer — *mon Dieu*.

Going from the ridiculous to the sublime, in the final match in Group A, Senegal and Uruguay produced arguably the finest game of the tournament. Senegal came out, as they had earlier against France, looking to blow their opposition off the park with fierce, attacking football and led 3–0 at half-time, thanks to a double from Papa Bouba Diop. Uruguay had battled well in their other games but seemed to have nothing up-front. A desperate Uruguayan coach Victor Pua sent on Morales and Forlan at half-time in an effort to salvage the seemingly hopeless situation — but was he playing with fire?

Morales scored virtually from the kick-off. Suddenly, Uruguay were free to attack, and the transformation was dazzling. They hammered Senegal, who were made to look pedestrian by comparison, and with twenty minutes left in the match, Forlan scored a second to bring them within a goal. Misses by Forlan and Silva seemed to have sealed their fate until, with two minutes left in the game, Recoba scored from the penalty spot to equalise at 3–3. As the game went into injury time, Rodriguez hit a thunderous volley that was blocked by Senegal's full-back, Diatta. The ball ballooned up to giant striker Morales who proceeded to head the ball wide from two metres out. So near, and yet so far. Senegal and Denmark were through to the next round. And the shocks just kept on coming.

Group B got off to a flyer with an exhilarating 2–2 draw between South Africa and a Paraguayan team led by the ageless Chilavert and coached by Italian Cesare Maldini. Spain played strongly in their opening match to defeat Slovenia, 3–1. The Slovenians tried hard but looked outclassed across the park. Spain then met Paraguay five days later and gave them a hiding, 3–1. With two goals to Fernando Morientes, the Spanish were swaggeringly good, but they had flattered to deceive so many times before that for most pundits it was still a case of 'wait and see'. South Africa then pipped tiny Slovenia 1–0 to set up an enthralling finish to the group. The South Africans had four points and Paraguay, one. Even if South Africa lost and Paraguay won in the final matches, Spain would have to drill the South Africans in order for Paraguay to go through on goal difference.

Spain and South Africa turned on a thriller, with the Spanish keeping their early average up and scoring another three goals to defeat South Africa. But the South Africans were not disgraced, with two goals of their own. The equation for Paraguay was simple — to qualify, they needed victory by a clear two goals.

Things started badly for them in the match against Slovenia when Carlos Paredes was sent off after twenty minutes, and then got worse, when an error by Chilavert gifted the Slovenians with a goal moments before half-time. The second half began where the first had left off, with Slovenia, led by Acimovic, peppering the Paraguayan goal. Paraguay were in a bind; with only ten men on the field they were flat out just to defend but, unless they scored three times inside half an hour, their tournament was over.

In the sixty-first minute, Maldini sent on striker Nelson Cuevas with immediate effect. Looking a bit like a frantic, over-wound toy, Cuevas collected the ball on the right, cut inside, and drilled his shot past goalkeeper Dabanovic to level the score at 1–1. Ten minutes later, Campos scored to make it 2–1 to Paraguay. With just ten minutes to go before full-time, Slovenia collected a red card and suddenly Paraguay were right back in the game — but would they have time to find the third goal they needed? The answer came five minutes later through another goal to super-sub Cuevas, and Paraguay had sealed an improbable victory to join Spain in round two.

Group C was a carbon copy of Group B, with the top team, Brazil, winning all three games and thereby making the battle for the other place in second phase a nail-biter. The Brazilians kicked off the group with a solid win against a Turkish team that surprised everyone with just how ready they were for World Cup football. The Turks really took the game to Brazil and were probably a bit unlucky to go down 2–1, but it was the antics of Rivaldo late in the game that soured the night for everyone.

In the last seconds of the game, Turkish defender Hakan Ünsal kicked the ball to Rivaldo for the Brazilian to take a corner. The ball was kicked with unnecessary venom but it was still fairly innocuous. As the ball struck his thigh, Rivaldo threw himself to the ground, clutching at his face and writhing in agony as if he'd been shot. The referee was fooled and Ünsal was given a red card. At this stage, the match was effectively over and Brazil were in no danger of losing, so Rivaldo's performance seemed even more cynical and ugly than had the result been up for grabs. Still, Brazil looked imperious in passages and sent an ominous warning to their rivals.

Not all of the tournament debutants started as well as Senegal. China began with a 2–0 loss to Costa Rica, boasting Paulo Wanchope (possibly the most unco-looking man in football). They then followed up with a 4–0 thrashing from Brazil. Turkey had probably become second-favourites in the group after their strong showing against Brazil, but, surprisingly, in their next game Costa Rica held them to a 1–1 draw to set up a make-or-break last couple of games. Either Turkey or Costa Rica could go through to the next round with Brazil, depending on the results.

The Turks returned to their early form against the disappointing Chinese and won 3–0, with a brilliant Hasan Sas scoring one goal and creating the other two, while Costa Rica dropped their bundle in a goal-fest against Brazil, going down 5–2, thanks mainly to some truly diabolical finishing.

Brazil had dominated the group with eleven goals and looked spectacular, but for many neutrals the lasting impression of the group was of Rivaldo getting a player sent off, out of sheer, malicious opportunism. Having for so long been the target of cynical and unsportsmanlike attempts to curb the Brazilian beautiful game, it was a moment of perverse irony to see a Brazilian revert to this sort of cheating. I must confess that, as much as I am a fan of Rivaldo's genius, I've never looked at him the same way since that night against Turkey in Ulsan.

Group D began with another of the pre-tournament favourites, Portugal, opening their campaign against a seriously outgunned USA. The only problem was that the USA seemed unaware of the hopelessness of their task, and within thirty minutes they had put Portugal's World Cup aspirations on life support. Goals to McBride and O'Brien plus an own goal to Costa gave them a 3–1 advantage at half-time. Figo's golden generation rallied in the second half but could do no better than a 3–2 loss. Disaster.

Co-hosts South Korea, under the direction of Guus Hiddink, came out to rapturous support and racked Poland 2–0. Portugal picked up the pieces of their game and proceeded to take out their frustrations on the hapless Poles, 4–0, thanks mainly to a hat-trick to Pauleta. Then the USA and South Korea played out a businesslike draw to set up a finale in which anyone but Poland could win the group.

All the pressure was on Portugal, and it showed. Needing only a draw against South Korea, they collectively lost the plot and had two players sent off (Jao Pinto, for hitting the referee) and lost 1–0. Whereas the French had simply failed to turn up, Portugal had committed football harakiri. In the other must-win match, Poland finally awoke and blitzed the USA 3–1, but to little effect, as South Korea and the USA went through, and seriously warm favourites Portugal were out.

Group E was a strange assortment of football extremes. There were the ruthlessly efficient Germans, everybody's second-favourite team, Cameroon, a pretty anonymous Saudi Arabia, and an Irish team that had, under Jack Charlton, cast off their reputation for romantic failure to become football's equivalent of a seaweed invasion on a summer's day — really annoying and impossible to get through. Now under the direction of new coach Mick McCarthy, Ireland had a strong squad led by Manchester United's brilliant midfielder Roy Keane. But in one of the many strange twists to the saga of Keane's life, the captain was sent home from the tournament after a very public fight with McCarthy at a

pre-tournament team camp, over the coach's attitude to everything from global warming to his preference in underwear.

First up, the Irish met Cameroon, whose new strip made them
look like an Olympic 4 x 100 metre relay team that had turned up
at the wrong venue. A spirited affair ended in a 1–1 draw, with
which everyone seemed content. Germany and Saudi Arabia
played out an eight-goal thriller in Sapporo. Unfortunately, the
Germans scored all eight goals, making things substantially less
thrilling for the Saudis. Germany found the going a little tougher
next game against Ireland, who put in a performance straight out
of the old Jack Charlton playbook to hold the Germans, 1–1, in a
match they could easily have won.

Once again, the group was almost wide-open going into the
final round of matches. The Irish needed to win to stay alive,
while Cameroon knew that a draw would be good enough to see
them through. Germany put an end to the African nation's dream,
winning an ill-tempered match in which both teams had a player
sent off and sixteen yellow cards were handed out, 2–0. Striker
Miroslav Klose was in rare form but this was mitigated by the fact
that midfield *übermensch* Michael Ballack was clearly carrying an
injury and was well below his best. Meanwhile, the Irish finally
decided to take some chances and whacked three goals past Saudi
Arabia, who then joined France and China in the dubious group
to exit without scoring a goal. Ireland and Germany were into the
round of sixteen.

Group F had formally identified itself as the group of death.
Made up of England, Sweden, and Nigeria, along with tournament favourites Argentina, there were no weak teams or soft
games. The Swedes came prepared for this level of competition,
having had what used to be called a spirited preparation in the lead
up to the tournament. It was so spirited, in fact, that Mellberg and
Ljungberg came to blows during a five-a-side drill at training.

Thankfully, by the time they met England, under the direction of fellow Swede Sven-Goran Erikson, they had got it out of their system and the two teams played out an absorbing 1–1 draw. On the same day Argentina beat Nigeria 1–0, in a match in which they could easily have had five.

The Swedes then beat Nigeria, 2–1, with Larsson bagging two, and again it looked as though the world had seriously under-rated the teams from Scandinavia. In the match of the group, Argentina met England in Sapporo. The destinies of these two teams at the World Cup seemed constantly intertwined, like star-crossed lovers — except that they hate each other. In a commanding display, England defeated the more favoured Argentines by a solitary goal to David Beckham, achieving some measure of revenge for '86 and '94.

In the final matches, only Nigeria was out of the running for a place in the second phase. Argentina met Sweden knowing that a win was vital. The Swedes were content to sit back and defend; they allowed Argentina to dominate territory and possession, and Argentina played into their hands with abysmal finishing. Somehow, one minute before half-time, Claudi Caniggia created history by being red-carded for dissent while still on the bench. Then, ten minutes into the second half, disaster struck, when Svensson curled a free-kick inside the post to give the Swedes a 1–0 advantage. Argentina could not find an equaliser, until, with less than five minutes in the game, they had a penalty awarded. Ortega's spot-kick was saved by keeper Magnus Hedman, but Hernan Crespo leapt on the rebound to level scores at 1–1. As the final whistle sounded moments later, and the news filtered in that England had played out a dull 0–0 draw with Nigeria, the unthinkable was confirmed. The image of Battistuta sitting, weeping on the bench at full-time said it all: another giant had fallen, Argentina were out of the World Cup.

Group G began with a better-than-expected Mexico defeating a worse-than-expected Croatia 1–0. The other group match went exactly to form when Italy beat Ecuador 2–0, with Vieri looking menacing. But five days later the group was turned upside-down when Croatia beat the fancied Italians 2–1. There were some contentious refereeing decisions that did seem to go mainly against Italy but they were peripheral to the result at best. The Italians' problems seemed to stem from the fact that they were defending too deep and in too great numbers and then, on the rare occasions when they went forward, their finishing was poor. Coach Trapattoni's tactics did not seem to suit the players he had at his disposal. Mexico continued to defy expectations and beat Ecuador 2–1 to clinch their place in the second phase.

In the final matches for the group, Italy drew with Mexico 1–1, allowing both teams to qualify. Del Piero scored the equaliser for the *Azzurri* with barely four minutes remaining after Borgetti's wonderful first-half goal had put Mexico in front. Croatia tried but just couldn't reproduce the magic of '98 and went down to Ecuador 1–0, thanks to a goal from Mendez in the opening minutes of the second half.

In the final group, Russia put in a strong performance to beat Tunisia 2–0 while home-team Japan got their campaign off to the right start with an entertaining 2–2 draw with Belgium. They may not have registered on the radar of football's superpowers but, playing in front of a supportive home crowd, Japan looked like they could damage some egos. And damage them they did, with a precious 1–0 victory over Russia at Yokohama International Stadium four days later. Tunisia came to the party, holding Belgium to a surprise 1–1 draw, which left Japan, Russia, and Belgium with the same, simple task: win the final game and you're in the second round.

Some teams are overwhelmed with the expectations of their

fans, but Japan were riding an incredible wave of support. In Osaka, the urgency of their play brushed Tunisia aside and paved the way for a 2–0 win, sending Japan through on top of their group. In the other match Belgium began well, taking the game to the Russians with an early goal through a magnificent twenty-five-metre free kick from Johan Walem. The rest of the first half was a pretty even struggle but in the second half the game broke open after Bestschastnykh equalised for Russia. Twenty minutes later Wesley Sonck restored Belgium's lead and five minutes after that Belgian captain and man-of-the-match Marc Wilmots made it 3–1 to Belgium. Russia got a late consolation goal but it wasn't enough to stop Belgium joining Japan in the second round.

What the first round of Korea/Japan might have lacked in quality football, it more than made up for in upsets and controversy, both on and off the field. The elimination of France (the defending champion), Portugal, and (perhaps most surprisingly of all) Argentina were nothing short of sensational. In contrast, the form of Senegal, Japan, USA, and South Korea was an unexpected source of joy. The standard of refereeing was generally poor and inconsistent, provoking a stern response from FIFA midway through the group stage. Two trends to emerge clearly were that many of the European teams seemed tired and stale, while the unbridled enthusiasm of some of the lesser lights was proving to be a vital ingredient in a very different style of tournament.

As the after shocks from round one subsided, the round of sixteen shaped up as follows:

Round Two

Germany vs Paraguay	Denmark vs England
Sweden vs Senegal	Spain vs Ireland
USA vs Mexico	Brazil vs Belgium
Japan vs Turkey	Italy vs South Korea

The second round began with a return to tradition. Germany were methodical and workmanlike in grinding out a 1–0 victory over Paraguay. The South Americans were unimpressive and seemed flat and one-paced, as they had been for the entire tournament with the exception of twenty-five minutes against Slovenia when super-sub Cuevas had set them alight. Inexplicably, with the entire tournament to play for and trailing 1–0, coach Cesare Maldini waited until there was barely sixty seconds of playing time left to bring on match-winner Cuevas. I named the 'Cesare Maldini: what was I thinking?' award in honour of this moment.

England destroyed Denmark 3–0 in their most impressive display so far. It was virtually one-way traffic and with the early departure of three tournament favourites, the English began to firm as possible contenders. The next day Senegal met Sweden in an enthralling match that was eventually decided by a 'golden goal' after being locked at 1–1 at full-time. Senegal, the sentimental favourites, finally out-enthused the Swedes to find themselves, unbelievably, in the quarter-finals.

Spain and Ireland went at each other in a thrilling encounter at Suwon with the game being, again, locked at 1–1 after extra time. This time, however, it went to penalties where Spain won out 3–2, but it was the sort of game that made you sorry there had to be a loser. Mexico met their CONCACAF rivals USA in a match the form guide told you should have been a gimme for the Mexicans. Unfortunately for them, that form guide had been thrown out the window on day one of this tournament, and the USA triumphed 2–0 with tournament revelation Landon Donovan and Brian McBride scoring.

Brazil were drawn to meet the most over-achieving team in the history of world football: Belgium. Led by Marc Wilmots, the Belgians were well organised and as a team played well above their talent as individuals. They came out against Brazil and showed they were here to win it from the opening whistle. Then, just before half-time, Wilmots controlled the ball in the area and turned and shot in one motion — goal! But no, it was disallowed for handball, despite the video proving once again inconclusive. Brazil scored twice in the second half, through Ronaldo and Rivaldo, to take their place in the quarter-finals and leave the Belgian fans to play 'if only' for the next four years.

Having already played out of their boots to get this far, co-hosts Japan met tournament sensations Turkey and immediately looked outclassed. In the end, Turkey got them 1–0 but in truth the Japanese were always struggling to get into the game.

The other co-hosts, South Korea, met Italy in the final match of the round of sixteen, a game both countries are still talking about. Once again, the Italians sat back, defended too deep and refused to attack the Koreans. And also once again, they appeared to be on the wrong end of a number of key decisions by the referee.

Vieri was left isolated at the front without any midfield or forward support. Nonetheless he was able to put the *Azzurri* ahead 1–0 after seventeen minutes. But Italy would not come forward to consolidate their lead and eventually their tactics backfired when Seol Ki-Hyeon equalised in the dying minutes of play. Even in extra time the Italians stuck to their defensive structure and paid dearly when Ahn Jung-Hwan scored a 'golden goal' to eliminate them from the tournament. For his troubles Jung-Hwan was promptly dumped by his Italian club side, Perugia, for insulting Italian football by scoring the goal that eliminated them from the World Cup!

As the Italians tried to digest the unthinkable, Vieri spoke out against Trapattoni's tactics, asking 'why were we sitting back against South Korea, why didn't we try to win?'. Good question. But it was all too late for the Italians, and another giant had fallen.

For the first time in World Cup history, the quarter-finals would include a team from Europe, Asia, Africa, and both North and South America. They began with a pedigree, heavy-weight, main-event clash: Brazil vs England. Throughout the tournament Brazil had run hot and cold, looking brilliant at times and struggling at others. England had seemed strong while hinting that their best football was in front of them as their campaign gained momentum. Ultimately, the match would pose more questions than it answered.

England began well and were rewarded for some creative and attacking play when, in the twenty-second minute, Michael Owen scored to give them a perfect start. But now Brazil began to come into the game, controlling the rhythm of play with Ronaldhino as conductor. Finally, after a minute of extra time at the end of the first half, he was able to contrive a goal for Rivaldo, to send the teams in at half-time level at 1–1. The English were gutted.

The second half began with everyone waiting on England's response, but nothing came. Before they could build any momentum, Ronaldhino stopped them in their tracks with the goal of the tournament. From an apparently non-threatening position, wide on the right, he curled in a drifting, dipping shot that left English keeper David Seaman mesmerised as it lobbed over his head and dropped into the net. Was it intended as a cross or a shot? All that mattered was that it was a goal and Brazil led 2–1.

Surely now England would come to life. Their formation had seemed a little rigid and inflexible even in victory. Now it seemed positively straight-jacket material. All of a sudden Ronaldhino was sent off for a foul on English defender Danny Mills. With half an hour left to play this was England's big chance. Coach Eriksson's response? Steady as she goes, sit back and wait for something to happen. And sure enough it did: England lost 2–1, and to this day that lost thirty minutes of opportunity remains mystifying.

The same day, Germany met the USA in Ulsan. The Germans withstood a spirited effort from the Americans to come away with a 1–0 win thanks to a goal from Michael Ballack. It hadn't all been plain sailing though, and Germany probably owed their victory to Oliver Kahn, who had a great day in goal with several fine saves.

Next day, Spain played South Korea and again it was a match plagued by controversy. They say you need an ounce of luck to win a World Cup; well, Korea had it in spades right through the tournament. Make no mistake: they worked hard, they trained hard, and they never surrendered on the pitch. But they also had the rub of the green and, in this tournament, that meant everything. 0–0 after extra time and South Korea through to the semi-finals, 5–3 on penalties. Shock level? 8.2 on the Richter Scale.

In the last quarter-final Senegal met Turkey and, probably due to the enormity of the occasion, the Senegalese played cagey and ultimately couldn't pull it off against the very impressive Turks. It took a 'golden goal' from Ilhan Mansiz to beat them, but the Lions of Terranga would go home as heroes to millions of people around the world.

The semi-finals matched Germany with the South Koreans and, for the second time in the tournament, Brazil with Turkey. So far the tournament had been dangerously unpredictable; now it settled down to follow the script.

While everything had been going to hell around them, the Germans had been a model of Teutonic regularity. Their campaign so far had rested on captain Oliver Kahn in goal and Michael Ballack in the midfield, and the semi-final was a case of more of the same — only with an evil twist for German fans. Sure enough, they got the expected victory 1–0 over South Korea with Kahn keeping another clean sheet and Ballack scoring the goal. But on top of that, Ballack picked up a second yellow card and would miss the final. With Ballack in the midfield, the Germans were efficient, impossible to break down, and capable of moments of real inspiration. Without him they looked outgunned.

After the theatrical efforts of Rivaldo in their first meeting, the Brazil vs Turkey semi-final was always going to be a tense encounter. Brazil won it, thanks to a goal from Ronaldo in the last seconds of the first half, and marched into the final to meet Germany. At the business end of the tournament, they looked dominant and menacing, in equal measure.

Strangely, for a tournament that had seen so many underdogs perform so well, the final came down to a clash between the two most successful nations in World Cup history. Ollie Kahn had an off day by his standards and Brazil had a good one by theirs, with two goals from tournament top-scorer Ronaldo late in the second half. Germany managed to hit the woodwork a couple of times — one effort by Oliver Neuville was particularly spectacular — but somehow you felt that the match had been decided as soon as Ballack was suspended five days earlier.

Brazil lifted the World Cup trophy for a fifth time and most would agree that it had been a marvellously dramatic, controversial, and entertaining tournament. Maybe it wasn't one for the football purists, but it had turned on theatre of the highest quality to prove, above all, that football is a broad church with many rooms in the mansion.

COMETH THE HOUR

Great World Cup Moments

Each person finds their own heroes and villains at the World Cup. Sometimes they are shared by the general public, like Senegal in 2002 or Croatia in 1998. Others may be specific to you alone (and, simultaneously, half a million other people around the world). Part of the magic is that the tournament throws together wild combinations of teams with different styles of play and different strengths and weaknesses in a high-pressure, combustible environment. It is the greatest living, working model of the 'scissors, paper, rock' principle on the planet. For me, it's the team and individual performances that come out of left-field which create the theatre of the tournament. Some rise to the occasion while others are crushed like insects by the sheer weight of events. And then there is that special class of individual who seems unnaturally blessed or cursed by the gods and is forced to act out the whole epic on the biggest stage in the world. Here are a few of my favourites that have fuelled my love for the game over thirty-six years.

Round One, USA 1994, Giants Stadium, New York
ITALY vs REPUBLIC OF IRELAND

I have always loved Italian football, but I am Australian of Irish/English grandparents and so I feel a natural affinity for the boys in green. I've spent a lot of time and have watched a lot of football in both Ireland and Italy, so I know first-hand what it means to both sets of fans. When the two teams met in the first round of USA 1994, Italy were tournament second-favourites and setting themselves for a long campaign and a tilt at winning the whole shemozzle. Ireland were still basking in the summer of the Jack Charlton renaissance — but it was very late summer and the autumn winds were starting to blow. The Italians were absolute thoroughbreds. Their attack of Baggio, Signori, and Vialli was worth enough cold, hard cash to buy the entire Irish squad — an ageing bunch of first- and second-division players — three times over.

The match kicks off and we all sit back for what we expect will be the usual slog of 'can the skilful Italians break the dour Irish down?' when, out of nowhere, Irish midfielder Ray Houghton scores with a wonder-goal. With eighty minutes still left on the clock, this changes everything. Now, one of the great chapters in football's Illiad begins to unfold... But the hero of the day wasn't to be one of the Italian superstars, but a thirty-five-year-old Irish defender named Paul McGrath.

McGrath was a jack-of-all-trades defender/midfielder for Ireland, Manchester United, and Aston Villa. The first black Irish captain, McGrath was raised in an orphanage in Dublin. When he retired finally in 1998 he had played seventeen years of top-flight football, and when he took the field at USA '94, he had already had thirteen knee operations (yes, thirteen!) and was an alcoholic, battling his disease. The combination of alcohol and injury meant that he had not been able to train for club or country in full-field drills since 1989 but was restricted to gym work. In short, Paul McGrath was a man for whom life started out tough and then pretty much stayed that way.

As the game unfolded, the Italians probed and pressured in search of a goal. In a match they were expected to win easily on account of the sheer difference in class their stable of elite goal-scorers could not create an equalizer.

The Irish, to a man, defend heroically, but even in this company, McGrath is a colossus. With McGrath blanketing him, Baggio simply cannot get a kick. In one sequence, McGrath slide tackles a pass off Baggio's toes on the edge of the box. The ball is chipped straight back in the air and McGrath climbs off the ground to win the header. He falls, just in time to take a returned half-volley straight in the face and, without blinking, he climbs to his feet and races out to recover the loose ball.

That day at Giants Stadium will live long in the hearts and minds of Irish fans. Paul McGrath was courage, intelligence, and cool presence of mind personified. It wasn't just that he negated a great attack. His ability to play forward out of defence and create something in midfield meant that the buck stopped with him all day, keeping the pressure on the Italians and preventing them from building the sort of cohesive forward momentum that produces goals.

Today, most commentators will agree that McGrath is one of the greatest to have worn the green and white, and Aston Villa fans remember him simply as 'God', but when people sing the praises of 'the black pearl of Inchicore', it is this game that typically pro-vokes the superlatives. And if for nothing else, Australian cricket fans should remember him when they appropriate the song that was written in his honour: '*Ooh — aah Paul McGrath, Ooh aah Paul McGrath.*'

Round One, France 1998, Stade Lescure, Bordeaux
ITALY vs CHILE

Much of the cruel beauty of football lies in the fact that it is a game of moments, and that at any given moment you have the chance to succeed or fail in a way that will obliterate everything you ever did before. One tiny error can wash away the reputation of a cham-pion and you never get the chance to go back and rewrite history. When Roberto Baggio famously missed the fifth and decisive penalty in the final of USA '94, no one remembered 'Baggio the champion' and the fact that he had scored five goals in the knockout phase of the tournament to single-handedly get the Italians into the final, or that he had carried a hamstring injury for the entire match, or even that two of his team mates also missed penalties before him. Instead, Baggio is tagged as the man who, in front of the largest TV audience in history, meekly handed the World Cup to Brazil by missing the all-important fifth spot-kick.

Four years later at France 1998, Italy were drawn in one of the toughest first-round groups, alongside Cameroon, Austria, and Chile. The *Azzurri* have been notoriously slow starters at big tournaments, but at the World Cup early results are crucial because, apart from helping you to build confidence and momentum, where you finish in the group stage determines who you will play in the elimination rounds. So, they went into their first group match against Chile knowing this was a must-not-lose game for both teams.

In any other year, Italy vs Chile might seem like a no-brainer, with Chile being delighted to get away with a 0–0 draw, or perhaps even 1–1 if they scored first. But 1998 was not like any other year, and Chile boasted a seriously competitive team based around two great strikers — Salas and captain Zamorano. Both were lethal finishers, both combined well, and both were in dangerously good form coming into the tournament.

As the match got underway, Italy took an early 1–0 lead through Christian Vieri, but then, as is often the way with the *Azzurri*, they sat back and looked to control the game. The scoreboard will tell us that they did this successfully until the end of the first half, when, in the last minutes of play, Salas scored for Chile. If the Italians were thinking of a draw they were shocked when, five minutes into the second half, Salas repeated the dose, and suddenly they were a goal behind in the vital opening game of the tournament. Obviously, they needed a second goal to stay alive but this had to be balanced against the fact that if Italy left themselves open and conceded a third goal then there would be no way back.

The minutes ticked away but no goal came, creating greater and greater pressure on the increasingly desperate Italians. Then, with five minutes remaining, Chile conceded a penalty. The crowd held its breath as it waited to see who would take this all-important spot-kick to save the entire Italian World Cup campaign. Without hesitation, up stepped Roberto Baggio.

Many will tell you that on this afternoon, four years after the final in Los Angeles, Baggio had still not entirely recovered from the dramatic final at USA '94. Not many people are given the opportunity to stand at the top of their known world and survey all around them — imagine getting one step away from that only to lose your balance and fall.

As Baggio stepped up to place the ball, even the most hardened journalists could hardly bring themselves to watch. One wondered, if he missed would there be anywhere left for Baggio to go? Could anyone survive this sort of setback twice?

Finally, he moved in, striking the ball low and to the keeper's right. Guessing correctly, the goalie flung himself low, towards the right corner — but to no avail. Goal! Roberto Baggio had returned from the wastelands of the World Cup in the most emphatic and courageous manner. History records that Italy snatched a draw against Chile via a late penalty, but for those fortunate enough to witness the moment, it was so much more than that.

Italy 1990
CAMEROON vs THE WORLD

Italia '90 was a tournament remembered for all the wrong reasons: negative football, cynical fouls, time wasting, diving, and a final won on a dubious penalty — yuk! However one man almost single-handedly rescued the tournament for the romantics and lovers of the beautiful game. That man was Roger Milla, from Cameroon.

Milla's unlikely career at international level got off to a conventionally great start when he scored on debut in 1978. He quickly became famous in Africa for his feats at African clubs Eclair Douala, Leopards of Douala, and Tonnerre of Yaounde. Surely it was just a matter of time until the big, international contract arrived (although this was still something of a rarity in Africa in the '70s). But the big deal never came and when Europe finally beckoned it was only with the promise of lower-division football at a fraction of the money he could have expected — a tale that will be familiar to many African footballers even today. Milla plugged away without ever getting the big break, collecting a second-division championship with St Etienne in France and enjoying representative football as a member of Cameroon's 1982 World Cup side. Finally, in 1987, he retired from international football, with a lot of unfulfilled hopes as his main legacy.

Following Cameroon's qualification for the World Cup finals in 1990, the president of Cameroon rang Milla to plead with him in person to come out of retirement. 'Oh well,' said Milla, 'What are you gonna do?' (or something like that), and joined the Indomitable Lions for their campaign in Italy. And things started well immediately at the opening match of the tournament in Milan, where they surprised everyone with a 1–0 victory over World Cup–holders Argentina, despite having two players sent off. But still, the general feeling was that Cameroon had got the disappointing Argentines on a bad night and they could expect a tougher game against Romania.

They met Romania on 14 June in the seaport town of Bari and the two sides were pretty evenly matched, with neither able to manufacture an advantage. Then, fifteen minutes into the second half, thirty-eight-year-old Roger Milla was substituted on, and everything changed. Within twenty minutes he had scored twice to defeat the stunned Romanians and ensure a place in the second round for Cameroon. This time it couldn't just be written off as good luck and the football world was forced to take the Lions seriously. Neutral fans around the world were warming to Cameroon's appealing style of play and, in particular, to Milla's unique goal celebration which involved jubilant dancing around the corner flag.

The round of sixteen saw them drawn to play another South American heavyweight, Columbia. In a tense and at times thrilling match, the teams remained locked together on 0–0 after the full ninety minutes. Once again, Milla came on as a late substitute and in the space of three, explosive minutes, late in extra time, he turned the game on its head. First, he beat two defenders to fire home a left-foot shot from a difficult angle and then, minutes later, after cheekily stealing the ball from wayward Columbian goal-keeper Higuita, he scored a second to put Cameroon into the quarter-finals. This was uncharted territory for an African nation at the World Cup and already, pundits were starting to talk about them reaching the final — and maybe even going one better. And why not? They were a young, fit, fast, and strong team and in Milla they had found a cool-headed talisman who simply could not miss in front of goal.

In the quarter-final they came up against a Paul Gascoigne–inspired England — daunting, but not impossible. The mood of the Indomitable Lions said 'bring it on, we fear no one'. The match fulfilled every expectation and produced one of the most entertaining encounters in World Cup history. England took an early lead and, in the first half, seemed to have the measure of their opponent. At half-time, super-sub Roger Milla was intro-duced and once again, things changed immediately. Suddenly his team-mates looked inspired as Milla, running at the English defence with the ball, provided a focus for the team's forward thrusts. Fifteen minutes into the second half, Milla was brought down in the penalty area and a spot-kick was awarded, which Kunde converted to level the scores at 1–1. Just four minutes later, Milla set up a nice one-two, to create an opportunity for Ekeke. He also scored, and suddenly Cameroon were in front, 2–1. England looked rattled.

But now the weakness of so many past African sides struck again. Cameroon's clumsy, brutal tackling presented England with two penalties which Gary Lineker cheerfully finished off to bring the Indomitable Lions' dream run to an end. As Milla trudged off the field he knew that while it had been an incredible ride, if they'd just kept their heads, Cameroon would have reached the final four of the World Cup at the very least.

But we hadn't seen the last of Roger Milla just yet. Four years later, he reprised his role as super-sub, coming on to score against Russia at USA '94 at forty-two years of age. His record, as the oldest goal-scorer in World Cup history, still stands. Age shall not weary them …

Round Two, Spain 1982, Estadio Sarria, Barcelona
ITALY vs BRAZIL

The second round match between Italy and Brazil in Spain 1982 has earned its place in the ten greatest matches of all-time purely for the quality football. As a game it had everything: contrasting styles, big name players, end-to-end football, heart-stopping drama, controversy … you get the picture. But beyond all that, it also saw one man act out the finale in his personal story of triumph, temptation, a fall from grace, and ultimately salvation. Redemption is at the heart of all great epics and this one had more drama than anything Cecil B DeMille ever dreamed up. It could

have starred Charlton Heston and been a box office smash — but
this one starred Paolo Rossi.

Going into the World Cup in 1982, Rossi was certainly the
most infamous player in world football. He had emerged from
Argentina '78 as the star of the promising young Italian squad and,
after being signed for a world record transfer fee, confirmed his
place as the darling of Italian football in the late '70s. He seemed
to have the world at his feet and then, like the biblical saga of
Lucifer, he was dethroned in an exercise of public humiliation that
perhaps only Maradona himself could rival. Rossi was charged
with match fixing, found guilty, and suspended from the all aspects
of the game for three years. This was eventually commuted to two
years on appeal and Rossi finally came back in from the cold a few
weeks before the end of the 1982 Italian season.

Italian fans and the football establishment were, by turns, aston-
ished and appalled when Italian coach Enzo Bearzot included him
in the World Cup squad for 1982. Bearzot smiled and said
nothing. In the first round of matches in Spain, Italy managed
three draws from three games, scoring a grand total of two goals,
neither of which belonged to Rossi. He also failed to score in their
second round match against Argentina. He looked slow, rusty, out
of touch, and thoroughly miserable but Bearzot persisted with
him, selecting him in all games despite the vitriolic criticism from
both the media and the fans. Some of the photos of Italian
training at the time seem to show Rossi looking as though he
couldn't believe that Bearzot could be this crazy.

In the second round, Italy came out to face Brazil in Barcelona.
The winner would progress through to the semi-finals of the
World Cup, the loser would go home. Meeting Brazil is never easy
especially in must-win matches, but the Brazilian team that took
the field that day at the Estadio Sarria was intimidating even by
Brazilian standards. With a midfield that included Zico, Socrates,

and Falcao they had *jogo bonito* coming out the kazoo and were unbackable favourites to win the tournament, let alone the match. Bearzot infuriated everyone, including his own parents, by selecting Paolo Rossi up-front yet again.

The match began with both teams nervous and out of rhythm. The pressure was enormous, the atmosphere tense and electric with the anticipation of something unique. With the game barely five minutes old, Italy's Oriali sprinted down the wing and then passed inside to Cabrini. Cabrini paused and then floated a delicate chip-cross to an unmarked Rossi who headed home to score with attitude plus. There was a stunned silence from all but the Italian fans. Italy 1, Brazil 0.

Brazil came forward looking for an equaliser and in doing so almost conceded a second, when Rossi created an opening, laying the ball off for Graziani, who missed a really good chance. The game was only two minutes old and already people were reaching for the nitroglycerine. Two minutes later Brazil's Serginho missed, with only Italian keeper Zoff to beat, and you knew it was going to be one of those games.

In the twelfth minute, Socrates received a pass on the edge of the box, dribbled it in, deceiving Zoff who came to meet him, and put his shot straight through between the keeper's legs. The Italian fans were clearly disappointed. They had come into the match as underdogs and to then take an early and unexpected lead, miss a sitter, and then concede an equaliser in the space of twelve minutes was more than anyone should have to take. On the other hand, the Brazilians looked so full of self-belief that you had the feeling that if they started with a three goal handicap it wouldn't make the slightest difference to their approach. Sixty seconds later and they were on the attack again through Zico. As he drifted through the box, Italian defensive nightmare Glaudio Gentile tried to kill him with something that vaguely resembled a tackle and collected a yellow card — and boy, did he have a collection. Gentile was like something that had stepped out of a Sergio Leone spaghetti western, but in his case it was no act. Nonetheless, to simply brand him a thug would be a huge underestimation of his ability as a footballer. He played in the vein of a classical Roman soldier, who simply did what his emperor asked of him. Throughout his career at Juventus, Gentile would show that he was a fine ball player and distributor with an ability to anticipate that was second to none.

Brazilian players and fans kept the samba going, while the Italians sat back, ever vigilant, waiting for the opportunity to deliver another sledgehammer blow. Ten minutes later it came. Under no pressure at all, Brazilian defender Leandro passed back to team-mate Cerezo who aimlessly lobbed a cross-field pass to no-one in particular. Pouncing like a true bird of prey, Rossi intercepted the ball and drove it past the hapless Brazilian keeper Peres. Italy 2, Brazil 1.

Now, for the first time, the merest hint of self-doubt was starting to show on the faces of the Brazilian team. In fact, close-ups of players on both teams reflected a growing sense that something bigger than your average football match was beginning to unfold. At home, all we could do was buckle-up and enjoy the ride. Moments before half-time, Brazil seemed to be denied an equalising penalty when Gentile almost ripped the shirt off Zico's back. Israeli referee Abraham Klein seemed to think it was just Gentile's traditional greeting and waved play on. Half-time came and people suddenly realised they hadn't exhaled for fifteen minutes.

The match resumed in the second half with both teams apparently aware that they would have to risk conceding in order to score, as time was running out. First Falcao, then Italian winger Bruno Conti, and finally Serginho missed good chances. Then

Junior got a ball inside to Cerezo who hit the upright. The tension had gone so far beyond unbearable that it was ridiculous. Finally, Falcao collected the ball on the edge of the Italian area. With a jink and a shimmy he was into the box and in space. With a final dummy he sent Zoff the wrong way before smashing the ball into the top corner — 2–2.

Momentum shifted back in Brazil's favour and they looked to have survived their momentary crisis of self-doubt. Surely now Italy were gone. Nobody could lead twice against such an extravagantly talented side and still get a result. With Italian blood in the water, Brazil closed in for the killer third goal. The scores remained level for exactly six minutes.

Italy were now playing what for them was all-out attacking football. Tordelli put in a corner that was cleared with the ball being redirected harmlessly into the Brazilian box towards a cluster of defenders in yellow shirts. Then, quicker than you can say buon giorno, Rossi appeared from nowhere, getting the slightest flick onto the ball and putting it into the net. The Brazilians just stood and stared like zombies in disbelief. It couldn't be happening, it just could not be happening. Rossi was ecstatic.

And that's how the scores remained: Italy 3, Brazil 2. Even the Italian fans felt sorry for Brazil. They were such a great team and, after the shenanigans of some of the other round one survivors, it seemed a cruel joke that the practitioners of the beautiful game were going home. But nobody said sport was fair.

Rossi's mercurial hat-trick captured the imagination of the football world and created the momentum that swept Italy to a tournament victory with, for once, the support of most neutrals. He went on to score three more goals in the elimination stage of Italy's campaign to help bring home the World Cup for the *Azzurri*. The fallen angel of Italian football had returned.

Semi Final, Mexico 1970, Estadio Azteca, Mexico City
ITALY vs WEST GERMANY

This was a classic from the moment it was confirmed. Two of football's heavyweights in a death or glory, winner take all clash. The Italian affair with *catenaccio* was at it's peak. Some called it ultra-defence and, in the hands of less skilful exponents of the art, that might be true. But the Italians were one of the finest teams in the world and used the strategy to control the pace of the game, maintaining possession and breaking the opponents' rhythm, to then strike with lethal efficiency. They had won the European Championship in 1968 doing exactly this and their leading domestic club, Inter Milan, was the scourge of European football.

West Germany were probably their equal but with a completely different philosophy. They were supremely fit, well trained, and highly technical. They had gone down in the final of the 1966 World Cup only after extra time and the most controversial goal in football history and since then had strengthened their squad considerably. Many neutrals consider the period between 1966 and 1974 (when they eventually triumphed in the World Cup) to be the German's greatest period ever.

The match was played in the stifling, midday heat of the Aztec stadium in Mexico. Both teams began slowly, feeling each other out and getting used to the difficult conditions. Suddenly the Italians sprang to life. Boninsegna played an elegant one-two with Riva and then, from sixteen metres, smashed an unstoppable shot past German keeper Sepp Maier. It had come out of nowhere and the Germans were stunned.

Falling behind 1–0 to Italy felt like 3–0 against anyone else thanks to the rigour of the *catenaccio* but West Germany were undaunted and upped the tempo of play to try and create an equaliser. It was creation with a small 'c', however, and more an act of sheer will power than artistry. But what they lacked in creative variety, they made up for with speed and stamina. With the brilliant duo of Beckenbauer and Overath guiding the way, they hammered away relentlessly at the Italian defence, launching attack after attack. But the Italians, under the leadership of Facchetti, soaked it all up and held firm. Grabowski and Müller had chances, and the ageing Seeler chased down everything, but at half-time the score was still 1–0 to Italy.

The second half served up more of the same with the Italians unwilling to risk anything on a serious attack. The Germans had already been forced to play into extra-time just three days earlier in a thriller against England, so time seemed to be on the side of the patient Italians. But the sustained pressure was starting to tell and in the sixty-fifth minute Müller dispossessed Albertosi and, with the keeper already beaten, Overath slammed his shot against the crossbar. Two minutes later came the pivotal moment in the match. Beckenbauer raced toward the Italian goal only to be cut down viciously by Cera. A definite penalty, surely — but the referee would have none of it and awarded a free-kick on the edge of the box.

It was only then that everyone noticed Beckenbauer, still writhing in pain on the ground. After examination by the medical team it was revealed that he had sustained a broken clavicle and dislocated his shoulder. The problem was that West Germany had used both of their two substitutions. In a display of courage that those who saw it will never forget, the Kaiser simply had his arm and shoulder taped rigid across his chest and returned to the field — in central defence, no less.

Still the Italians held on. The Germans were just too predictable in attack for this masterful defensive unit. Until in the very last minute of normal time, the ball was crossed in to Karl Heinz Schnellinger who drove it past Albertosi, to finally level the scores. The Germans were elated, the Italians devastated. The heat, the altitude, and the enormous act of discipline required to defend a lead for eighty-two minutes seemed to have taken its toll. They looked gone for all money.

Extra-time began with Müller collecting a tired back pass from Italian defender Poletti and firing it into the back of the net to give West Germany a precious lead after only five minutes. Suddenly the game, which had been so tight and controlled, exploded. The Italians were forced to go on the attack and they hit back three minutes later with Burgnich finishing an elaborate move to score: 2–2. But the Italians were not finished. Riva was their star striker, and probably the most feared goal-scorer in Europe, and now they finally managed to get the ball to him. Freed from his defensive commitments, he beat his marker and crashed the ball past Maier to restore Italy's lead, 3–2. Surely now it was over.

Players from both teams, fans, and officials were clearly exhausted by the conditions and the intensity of the match. The noise of over one hundred thousand cheering spectators was deafening. Still the Germans persisted in attack and after one hundred and ten minutes of play, Seeler headed the ball down to Müller who scrambled it over the line to again level the scores at 3–3. The German players were too tired to celebrate while their opponents simply hung their head in despair.

The match had transformed from a game of skill and strategy into a surreal endurance event. While most players were still struggling to comprehend what was happening the game re-started and straight from the kick-off the Italians got the ball to golden-boy striker Gianni Rivera. Rolling the ball in a manner very similar to Roberto Baggio nearly twenty-four years later, he made a bee-line for goal and slotted home the winner to seal the fate of the never-say-die Germans, 4–3.

The final whistle blew before play could be re-started and players collapsed into each other's arms and feel to the ground too exhausted to move. Both sides had given everything. It seemed as though the result was secondary to the epic drama of the battle itself.

Round Two, Mexico 1986, Estadio Nou Camp, Leon
BELGIUM vs USSR

As a match it had everything that makes football memorable: a mismatch, a tactical battle, all-out attack, changes in fortune, and finally a triumph against the odds for a team that didn't give itself a chance until ten minutes into the second half.

At first glance, this looked to everyone to be a mismatch of Anna Nicole Smith proportions. After the first-round matches of 1986 World Cup in Mexico there was one team everybody was talking about, the USSR. In the opening match they had beaten Hungary, who until then had seemed a good chance of making the semi-finals, 6–0 but it could easily have been 12–0. The Soviets scored from everywhere and played with such speed and precision that the Hungarians probably wished they hadn't qualified. The Soviets just went ballistic. In Belanov and Ratz they had two of the deadliest 25-metre-plus strikers in history, and this was in the days of the thirty-two panel leather balls not the Star Trek stuff that dips and swerves so unpredictably today. The USSR then drew 1–1 with France and then beat Canada 2–0 at a walk. They were simply awesome.

The Belgians, on the other hand, were under-whelming to say the least. They began by losing 2–1 to Mexico, struggled to beat Iraq 2–1, then drew 2–2 with Paraguay. They had so little confidence that they hadn't even bothered to arrange hotel accommodation after the first round and were confirmed on flights home the next day.

The match began pretty much as expected. The USSR attacked the Belgians with frightening ferocity. It was as if they had at least three extra players on the field and were intent on getting in five goals before half time. Plays swept from left to right and back again at unbelievable speed. The few times that a Belgian player was able to get the ball there was nobody to pass to, because the entire Belgian team was committed to last-ditch defence. Belgian goalkeeper Jean-Marie Pfaff looked up for the fight but the same could not be said for all of his team-mates.

Finally, after twenty-seven minutes, the inevitable happened. Igor Belanov cut across the edge of the box and pivoted in an almost inhuman display of flexibility to fire off a 25-metre special that shot into the goal like a Soviet surface-to-air missile. 1–0. The rest of the half continued much the same way, with Zavarov orchestrating the play in the midfield, the Soviets hit the post twice and put almost unbearable pressure on the Belgian defence. Pfaff left the ground at half-time to a standing ovation.

The second half began where the first had left off, with a Belanov header hitting the post and the Vervoort the Belgian full-back clearing off his own line. Then a subtle change began to creep over the game. The Belgians began to do a little attacking of their own. The Soviets had dominated the midfield with their short passing game. Now the Belgians began to play the ball to the wings and then cross it back to the centre, looking for the head of their 186-cm captain, Jan Ceulemens.

Belgium's main playmaker was the frustratingly inconsistent Enzo Scifo. While everyone knew he was capable of brilliance he had been virtually anonymous until now. Ten minutes into the second half, Frankie Vercauteren hit an innocent looking cross from deep on the left and, suddenly, there was Scifo who headed in the cross to level the scores. After one hour of almost total domination, the Soviet defence had fallen asleep and now found themselves level at 1–1.

The Belgians braced themselves for the backlash. It still seemed, for all the world, like a case of 'don't hit him back, you'll only make him mad' and sure enough the Soviets attacked from the re-start. Somehow they managed to run even faster and to work even harder, dazzling their opponents with the exception of Pfaff, who managed to defend his goal for a solid fifteen minutes.

Now both teams abandoned all pretence at tactics. It was an all-out attack. The battle raged from one end of the field to the other, and while the Soviets still looked awesome in attack they seemed vulnerable in defence, especially against the high ball. Belgium, on the other hand, seemed to get stronger as the game progressed.

For fifteen minutes both teams charged at each other like Bengal Lancers. The tension and excitement went right off the dial. Just as the possibility of a Belgian victory began to seem slightly less absurd, Belanov struck again. Running onto a through ball from Basily Ratz, he placed his shot past keeper Pfaff with surgical precision. It was 2–1 to the Soviets with 19 minutes remaining.

The heat and altitude of Mexico City had taken a tremendous toll on both teams, but particularly the USSR. They were exhausted. Their defence was leaden-footed and their mid-field had disappeared. They decided to put on their two substitutes, bringing on fresh legs to defend their lead. This proved to be a huge blunder. It meant they had no attacking players later when they really needed them.

The Belgians again began chipping away at the Soviet defence. Six minutes later Ceulemens collected a 50-metre pass on the edge of the Soviet penalty box. When he turned he found, to his utter astonishment, that no Soviet defender was bothering to challenge him. Three had managed to catch him in the offside trap but a fourth had not moved. Ceulemens took a stride and then beat the isolated keeper Dasaev. Score 2–2, with 13 minutes remaining.

Most members of the Soviet team were reduced to a walk, suffering extreme fatigue and oxygen deficit. The Belgians now looked metres faster and mentally much stronger. The Soviets hit the post. Then with two minutes remaining Dasaev made the save of the match to deny Enzo Scifo a second goal with a point-blank header at the far post. The exhausted Soviet defence had been unable to mark him and he arrived in perfect time to rise and nod in the header perfectly, only to be denied by the keeper. Even Scifo applauded.

As the players began the first period of extra time, the Belgians found themselves with two priceless advantages. First, they had not used either of their substitutes (which they now did). Second, they had twice come from behind to level the scores and so had a psychological edge over their exhausted and dispirited opponents.

The Soviets again rallied and attacked, but the Belgian defence held strong. Then in the seventh minute a Belgian counter-attack resulted in a corner kick. The Soviet defence stood and watched as yet another high cross sailed into the area, onto the head of Dasaev and into the Soviet goal. 3–2 to Belgium.

The Belgians sensed victory now and attacked in numbers. Panic had set in with the exhausted Soviets. Half of them were playing in fast-forward, half in slow-motion. In less than a minute a cross went straight past five Soviet defenders to Ceulemens on the left wing. He trapped the ball, turned, stopped and then accelerated, leaving his marker for dead. He crossed to Nico Clausens, who volleyed the ball past the keeper and into the net. Score 4–2 to Belgium.

Despairingly, Belanov urged his men on. With nothing to lose, the soviets threw everybody forward. Crosses and shots rained on the Belgian goal, but keeper Pfaf and his band of faithful defenders scrambled them away. Belanov flung himself at a cross, missed, and landed heavily on the ground. The referee awarded a penalty for a push in the back by a Belgian defender. Belanov scored: 4–3 to Belgium, and nine minutes to go.

Those nine minutes were the most exhausting I've ever endured as a spectator — but also the most exhilarating. In a last attack, Belanov managed to lose his marker and waited in space for the pass to come, with a virtually open goal beckoning. But the pass never came. Instead his team-mate tried to chip the ball over Pfaff and hit the crossbar. How poetic, how cruel. The referee blew his whistle and Belgium had pulled off perhaps the greatest comeback of all time. Players wept with joy, embracing each other as though they had just won the final. The Soviets were inconsolable, some hardly able to walk off the field. I still get goose-bumps just thinking about it.

FIVE
FLAVOURS
of
GENIUS

Technically, they were all perfect: control, passing, heading, shooting, the works. At their peak, they were all superb athletes, beautifully balanced and as graceful as gazelles, deadly as leopards, elusive as Tasmanian tigers. On top of that, each was gifted in a special way. I remember Pelé's anticipation, Best's almost magical ability to dribble and swerve at full speed, Beckenbauer's uncanny sense of when to inject himself into an attack, Cruyff's explosive acceleration and ability to 'read' a game, and Maradona's ability to destroy a defence single-handed with a running and passing game of unequalled brilliance.

Pelé

Pelé began his career in the mid-1950s as a shy teenager and ended it in the late 1970s as the founder and patron saint of the ill-fated American Soccer League. Along the way he collected two World Cup–final winners' medals (in 1958 and 1970), scored the greatest number of goals in history (over 1300), and was declared sports star of the twentieth century long before the century had ended. He was also labelled a national resource of Brazil (and therefore non-exportable). Not bad for kicking a ball around a park!

Born in the 'Three Hearts' district of the city of Santos, Brazil, Pelé's real name was Edson Avantes do Nascimento. The young Pelé's amazing skills were spotted while he was still playing bare-foot street football, and he was invited to join the Bauru Club. Later he moved to Santos which was his home club for almost his entire playing career. Despite reaching heights of wealth and acclaim that no other player has been able to equal, Pelé has never forgotten the poverty and hardship of his origins. His work for homeless and underprivileged children all over the world is legendary.

Word quickly spread of an outstanding new talent in Brazilian football, but it was not until the 1958 World Cup finals tournament in Sweden that most soccer fans and journalists saw what all the fuss was about. Pelé was the star of the tournament, and to shine in the midst of his champion team-mates Garrincha, Vava, Didi, Nilson Santos, and Djalma Santos required genius that was well beyond most international players. Pelé's World Cup debut at age seventeen coincided with Brazil's first World Cup victory and culminated in two goals in the final.

The young Pelé already had complete ball control, perfect footwork and incredibly wide peripheral vision. Perhaps more than any of these marvellous gifts, the thing that made the entire soccer world take Pelé to heart was the spirit of sheer, exuberant joy with which he played the game. Scoring a goal in his third successful World Cup final in 1970, he celebrated with all the enthusiasm of a nine-year-old playing in his first season.

He had courage too. One of the enduring images of world football must surely be the sight of Pelé, his face contorted by pain and frustration, being carried from the field during the Brazil versus Portugal World Cup tie in 1966. The greatest player on Earth had been savagely and methodically kicked out of the match. Needless to say, with him went Brazil's hopes of victory. In those days no substitutes were allowed, so ten minutes later Pelé reappeared, his legs a mass of bandages. Barely able to stand, he played out the remainder of the game. This is the picture that comes to my mind still when I hear the name 'Pelé'.

In a first-class career of nearly twenty-five years, Pelé scored 1363 goals, played 111 internationals in which he scored 97 goals, and helped his team win three World Cup finals. Along the way he became the best-known and best-loved popular figure in sport. At the twilight of his career he signed with the New York Cosmos, members of the fledgling North American Soccer League, and almost single-handedly popularised the sport in the USA. Since retiring he has become a tremendous ambassador for the game, as well as continuing his tireless efforts for the under-privileged children of the world. If that isn't enough, in 1994 he decided to take on the Brazilian FA to root out corruption in the game. He remains today, football's favourite ambassador and was voted the greatest player of all time at the end of the last millennium. Long live the king!

George Best

When it comes to scandals, public disgrace, tragedy and triumph in the daily press, there is one sports star who stands out like a beacon: George Best. If Diego Maradona, Paul Gascoigne, Eric Cantona and countless others have been victims of the nastiest kind of gutter journalism, George Best copped it first and worst. It was a whole new way to talk about a footballer. No one who followed football in the 1960s will ever forget him.

The late 1950s and early 1960s might have belonged to Brazil and Pelé, but from the mid-sixties to 1970 George Best was the superstar. He was more of an individualist then Pelé. His greatest skill was his dribbling; the ability to beat opponents by performing a series of feints, swerves and dummies using both feet, the ball, his body, his eyes, whatever — and all at a full sprint. Added to this, he was a lethal shot with both feet and an excellent header of the ball.

Off the field was another story altogether. While Pelé was the statesman of modern football, Best was the rascal; the rogue.

Like Pelé, Best came from humble beginnings. He was born on 22 May 1946 in Belfast, Ireland, where his father Dickie worked in the shipyards. One day in 1961, Manchester United's talent scout in Northern Ireland watched as his own son's team was annihilated by a tiny fifteen-year-old with the 'physique of a toothpick'. When he telegrammed Matt Busby at Manchester United, he didn't mince words: 'I think I've found a genius,' he said. How right he was. Best appeared in Manchester United's first-division side in 1964 and by the end of the season was a regular player. To appreciate the impact George Best had, we must remember that British football in the 1960s was dominated by the hard-running, high work-rate, all-purpose approach. Teams were very defensive, big on fitness, low on skill. Individually gifted players were considered a luxury.

At the same time, life in Britain was changing. Old ideas were being questioned and rejected. This youth revolution was led by pop bands like the Beatles, the Rolling Stones and the Animals — and by Georgie Best. By 1966 the press had taken to calling him 'the fifth Beatle'. The theme song of the era was 'My Generation' by the Who. It was an anthem of frustration against the boring, suffocating lifestyle of Britain in the early 1960s, expressed in the line 'hope I die before I get old'. Although George Best's message was sent out on the football field, it was the same. Bugger the boredom, let's take some risks and have some fun!

To fully understand his significance to the people of Northern Ireland in particular, you have to remember that during the late 1960s and early seventies, 'the troubles' were at their worst. Northern Ireland was occupied by the British army and suffering under years of sustained violence and real poverty and isolation. They were dark, hopeless days, and George Best provided a spark of relief and inspiration.

In 1968 Manchester United won the European Cup final and Best's display was galvanising. In the same year he was voted 'European Footballer of the Year'. It seemed that George could do no wrong.

If Best was the greatest sensation in British football on the field, his impact off it was no less amazing. His face could be seen endorsing everything from eggs and milk to bargain holidays and motor cars. His earnings off the field were more than ten times

his playing salary. He grew his hair long, he owned clothing bou-
tiques and nightclubs, he loved fast cars and beautiful women. He
was a swinger in every sense of the word.

To someone growing up in the twenty-first century, this kind
of lifestyle may not seem particularly unusual but when George
was doing it in the late 1960s he was doing it for the first time.
There had simply never been a sportsman like him — and the
golden age of English football owed almost everything to an
Irishman! Several sports journalists and many of George's team-
mates wondered aloud how long any player could keep up the
pace. George was besieged by the newspapers, agents wanting him
to put his name on things, women wanting to sleep with him,
women wanting to marry him, men wanting to buy him a drink,
men wanting to fight him … people even brought terminally ill
children to his house to see if George could cure them with his
touch. Added to this was George's showbiz lifestyle, late nights,
and heavy drinking.

It was during a League Cup tie with Manchester City in 1969
that the cracks began to appear for all to see. Best was booked for
kicking the ball away after the referee awarded a free kick against
United. Later, as he walked off the field, Best knocked the ball out
of the referee's hands — on national TV. Charge: bringing the
game into disrepute. Sentence: fourteen weeks suspension.

His first game back was an FA Cup tie against Northampton
Town. United won 8–2 with Best scoring six goals. His marker
that day, Roy Fairfax, later told the press, 'the closest I got to him
was when we shook hands at the end of the game'. A month later
he was sent off for spitting and throwing mud at the referee while
playing for Northern Ireland against Scotland. Sports journalists
and fans called it a bad patch, but it was more than that. Best's life
had reached terminal velocity. It was the beginning of the end.

George Best played thirty-seven times for Northern Ireland,

helped Manchester United win the League Cup twice in 1964–65 and again in 1966–67, and the European Cup in 1968. He was also voted European Player of the Year in 1968. He was United's leading scorer four times — but never appeared in a World Cup finals tournament. George Best was the most naturally gifted player I ever saw.

Much of his legend lives on in his oft-quoted sense of humour, which also hinted at the forces in his life that would ultimately kill him: 'I spent a lot of money on booze, birds and fast cars, the rest I just squandered'; 'If I had been born ugly, you would never have heard of Pelé'; and, commenting on his blood transfusion after a liver transplant to save his life: 'I was in for ten hours and had forty pints — beating my previous record by twenty minutes'.

Even as a new superstar emerged in the early 1970s, in the form of Johan Cruyff, Best's reputation endured. His Northern Ireland team-mate Derek Dougan said, 'Cruyff was manufactured on Earth. Georgie Best was made in heaven.' After a long and very public battle with alcoholism, George Best finally died of complications related to his disease in November 2005. On a dark and icy-cold winter's day, whipped by stinging Belfast rain, a crowd of several hundred thousand people lined the streets to farewell the Belfast boy.

Johan Cruyff

At the end of the 1960s, with George Best gone, things were looking pretty bleak for both players and fans of attacking soccer. Admittedly Brazil won the 1970 World Cup final with possibly the most perfectly balanced *jogo bonito* side ever but elsewhere it was a very different story. Coaches everywhere were falling over themselves to design new and more impenetrable eight-player defence systems.

Then, a miracle happened in the shape of a whippet-thin youngster with long hair, a hawkish face and an intense, passionate stare. His name was Johan Cruyff and he was born one street away from the Ajax club stadium in Amsterdam where his widowed mother worked as a cleaner. When Johan joined Ajax as a junior, the club helped her support her family. Again, we see genius flowering in the most difficult and deprived conditions.

In 1970, while Brazil was busy winning its third World Cup, a strange thing happened. A Dutch team won something! Feyenoord won the European Cup, the most prestigious trophy on the continent. Most people put it down to a fluke ... but over the next four years the Dutchmen showed how wrong they were.

In 1971 Ajax followed in Feyenoord's footsteps, winning the Dutch championship and then the European Cup. As a matter of fact, over the next four years there was precious little they didn't win. They were Dutch League champions 1970, 1972, 1973, Dutch Cup winners 1970, 1971, 1972, European Cup winners 1971, 1972, 1973, World Super Cup winners 1972, 1973, World Cup champions 1972. Meanwhile, Cruyff won the European Footballer of the Year award three times (1971, 1973 and 1974).

Cruyff was a player of extraordinary speed, balance, skill and intelligence. Where Best relied on his dribbling skills to defeat the close marking he was subjected to, Cruyff used his ability to accelerate and change direction at unbelievable speed. He seemed to glide everywhere effortlessly, using a stop-start-stop-start change of pace and direction that baffled the best defences in the world.

And it wasn't just Cruyff. The entire Ajax team seemed to be playing some weird sort of musical chairs. Players appeared in defence, then in midfield, back in defence again but on the left instead of the right — and then Cruyff would explode down the wing, beating tackle after tackle ... stop ... and then deliver a perfect high cross. It would be headed into the net by Neeskens or

Krol, who seemed to be playing both left-back and right-back as well as central midfield, but were in fact also playing the striker's role when they felt like it. Forget tactics, positions, formations. You might as well throw the book away altogether.

We've already talked about 'total football', the game plan where everyone did everything. Forwards defended, defenders attacked and everyone played midfield. The system relied on tremendous fitness and mental agility. But more than these, it relied on Johan Cruyff. He was the embodiment of the new ideal: total attack springing from total awareness.

The new kids in town were a wild bunch. Although the 1960s had left an indelible mark on everything, professional football had remained pretty insulated from the revolution. Footballers grew their hair (a little) and grew moustaches (a lot) but otherwise they were just as they'd been for decades. 'Straight' with a capital S!

Ajax players, or 'the Flying Dutchmen' as they were called, looked more like a rock band than a footy team. They wore long hair, and love beads, were rumoured to smoke marijuana, believed that sex was the best preparation for a big match, and listened to rock music in the dressing room. Their style of play was wild, brilliant and free-spirited and Cruyff was always at the centre of it.

Cruyff was also establishing a reputation for bitter confrontations with coaches, trainers and managers. Holland was still an emerging country in professional football, and Cruyff was paid a lot less than he would have got in Italy, Spain or Germany. There were many well-publicised clashes. In 1973 Johan Cruyff and Johan Neeskens were sold to Barcelona in Spain — a bombshell that some Ajax Amsterdam fans have still not totally recovered from. Cruyff's transfer fee was a world-record £1 million.

But in 1974 Cruyff and Neeskens returned to lead the Dutch World Cup challenge, and by now the whole football world was in a state nearing absolute panic about Cruyff and his fellow countrymen's brand of wizardry. Coaches were going blind watching slow-motion replays of the Dutch national team in action, searching for the secret behind 'total football'. But since there was no pattern to it, no one could find a formula to defeat it.

Anyone looking for an explanation of the mysteries at the heart of total football need go no further than the words of the great man himself: 'Speed is often confused with insight — when I start running earlier than the others, I appear faster'; 'Before I make a mistake, I do not make that mistake'; 'Every disadvantage has its advantage'; and his most famous saying: 'Coincidence is logical'.

In the early rounds of Germany '74, the Dutch didn't just beat their opponents, they thrashed them — first Uruguay, Sweden and Bulgaria; then Argentina, East Germany and Brazil. They scored fourteen goals and conceded just one. Their opponents in the final were the West Germans, the only other team with any claim to understanding total football.

The opening minute of the match remains one of the truly amazing stories of world soccer. Holland kicked off, passed the ball back through the midfield, seemingly doing nothing more than giving everyone a touch of the ball. Sixteen passes later, Cruyff collected the ball just inside the German half. He paused, then began tracking to the left, apparently aimlessly. Suddenly he darted forward, stopped, then darted again, losing his marker, and was inside the German penalty area in a split second. The Germans seemed to be moving in slow motion. At the last second a trip brought him down. Penalty. Neeskens converted and Holland led 1–0 after less than sixty seconds. The Germans had not even touched the ball! But West Germany went on to win the final 2–1. Dutch defender Rudy Krol remarked afterwards, 'You can score too quickly … You start thinking about the result instead of the match. We thought we were world champions. We woke up too late.' West German captain Franz Beckenbauer put things even more succinctly: 'He [Cruyff] was the better player, but I won the World Cup'.

Cruyff returned to club football with Spanish first-division team Barcelona, and continued to enhance his reputation. In 1975 he joined Pelé, George Best and Franz Beckenbauer in the United States. He played a couple of seasons in Florida, then returned to Holland. Although Holland qualified for the 1978 World Cup finals, Cruyff didn't join the team. He had retired from international football.

He kept on playing at a lower level with Feyenoord and with Ajax, finally retiring as a player in 1980. His record as a player was forty-eight internationals, producing thirty-three goals. In Dutch football he scored two hundred and fifteen league goals and in Spain he scored forty-seven with Barcelona.

Cruyff returned to Ajax in 1983 as a trainer and has gone on to become one of the leading coaches in Europe, winning titles with both Ajax and Barcelona. In 1994 his son made his debut with Barcelona. Cruyff was once asked if success as a coach made up for never collecting a winning finalist's medal in the World Cup. His answer was 'No,' followed by a brain-shrinking glare … 'of course not!'

Following heart surgery thanks to years of intense chain smoking, Cruyyf retired from coaching and now runs a foundation for under-privileged kids, amongst other interests. He still finds time to comment and agitate and polarise opinion about the world game.

Franz Beckenbauer: *der Kaiser!*

Franz Beckenbauer was born in West Germany in 1945 at the end of World War II. Life in a country ravaged by six years of war was hard. Again, we see a brilliant sportsman growing up poor. In interviews, Pelé, Best, Cruyff and Maradona all said that as children their only joy in life was a soccer ball. Beckenbauer first broke onto the world stage as a twenty-one-year-old in the 1966 World Cup. West Germany battled into the final to meet England, the host nation. In one of the most dramatic and controversial games in history, England eventually won 4–2 in extra time. Although he was on the losing team, Beckenbauer was quickly recognised as the new discovery in world football. He dominated the game, reading and dictating changes in direction and style constantly. He had great speed and ball control, as well as a lethal right foot. Starting off as a classic midfielder he opted to drop further back into the defence and became the greatest sweeper (or *libero*) in history. Like the other genius players, Beckenbauer always appeared to have time when in possession of the ball.

In the 1970 World Cup Beckenbauer was again in the limelight, this time as Germany's captain. First, he led his team to an unforgettable victory over England in the quarter-finals. In the revenge match of the century, Beckenbauer inspired his team to a 3–2 victory after England had led 2–0 at half-time. Then he led Germany into the semi-final against Italy, a team that was completely obsessed with ultra-defensive football. It was like the Great Wall of China, with eight players packed into the last third of the field. The key to victory for the Italians was to score first. They did, and for the next seventy minutes the Germans, led by Beckenbauer, ground away at the most disciplined defence in football history.

In the second half Beckenbauer was heavily fouled. Instead of getting up, he lay on the ground, writhing in agony with a dislocated shoulder. He was carried from the field but returned several minutes later with his right arm taped to his chest. The effect of his incredible display of courage was immediate. The Germans seemed suddenly to be fresher and faster than their opponents.

Finally, in the eighty-eighth minute, Schnellinger equalised, 1–1. As the final whistle sounded Beckenbauer collapsed on the grass, his face grey with exhaustion and agony. Extra time. In the heat and the altitude of Mexico, this was almost torture.

Germany scored first through Gerd Muller. 2–1. Italy, forced to attack in order to survive, equalised through full-back Burhnich. 2–2. Then Luigi Riva, Italy's lone attacker, scored with his cannon-like left foot. 3–2 to Italy.

With only minutes remaining, Beckenbauer launched a final attack. The Germans worked the ball downfield through the eleven Italian players and onto the head of Muller. 3–3. With two minutes to go, Giannini Rivera (who today is a member of the Italian parliament) scored directly from the kick-off to send Italy into the final and Germany to hell. Beckenbauer had again been on the losing side, yet he gave the world the greatest individual performance of the entire tournament.

In 1974 Franz finally got his winner's medal, defeating his rival Cruyff and the Flying Dutchmen. The 1970s proved to be a good period for Kaiser Franz all round. With Bayern Munich he achieved every honour in club football: league champions 1969, 1972, 1973, 1974; Cup winners 1969, 1971; European Cup winners 1974, 1975, 1976; World Champions 1976. He was also twice voted European Player of the Year, in 1972 and 1976. He then bowed out of international football, and in 1977 signed with the New York Cosmos. He finished his playing career with Hamburg in the early 1980s, retiring with the reputation of being West Germany's most complete footballer. By going onto a second successful career as West Germany's coach, Beckenbauer achieved the unique distinction of competing in three World Cups as a player (1966, 1970 and 1974) and three as a manager (1986, 1990 and 1994), and remains the only man to have won the World Cup as both captain and coach of his country.

Like Cruyff, he was dedicated, professional, but rather aloof. Perhaps these two players learned from the mistakes of George Best and others like him and made sure their lives were kept separate from the game. While his attitude to the press may at times have ruffled a few feathers, his impact on world football cannot be denied. Both as player and, later, as manager and coach, he has proved his brilliance time and time again. When he speaks, people listen, and the press hang on every word, whether it be criticism or praise. His presence in the German media has made him the face of the 2006 World Cup in Germany and the tournament's spokesman.

Maradona

If there was ever a player with precocious talent it was Diego Armando Maradona. His name, like George Best's, is synonymous with both genius and scandal. In the early 1980s he was Maradona, the God of Football: robust, athletic, mischievous, arrogant … astonishing. In the early 1990s he seemed more like a character from *Heartbreak High* or *Dallas* if Hunter S. Thompson had written the script — bloated, miserable, drug-ravaged … here was excess with a capital 'E'.

Diego Armando Maradona was born in Buenos Aires, Argentina, in 1961. He played his junior football with a local team known as 'the Little Onions'. Even at age ten the young Maradona showed a high level of skill as well as buckets of raw talent that marked him as a player of almost limitless potential. He was short but extremely strong, well-balanced and blisteringly fast. Almost exclusively left-footed, he was a magnificent striker of a dead ball as well as possessing a radar-like accuracy in passing. He played number 10 — the prize position — for his entire professional career.

By 1978 Maradona's achievements with Argentina's youth

teams had alerted the sporting media that the new prince was in town and in search of his crown. The same year he was selected in Argentina's World Cup squad. He was all of seventeen.

As training built up, the manager, Menotti, began cutting players to reduce the squad to a more manageable size. Then, in a shock announcement, Maradona was cut from the squad. (He was in fact the last player dropped.) Menotti announced to the world press that he decided to hold Maradona back and give him more time to mature. Maradona left the training camp in tears … a sight that would unfortunately become all too familiar in later years.

All the same, the four-year-delay before the next World Cup proved a godsend for Maradona's career. Clubs outside Argentina offered him astronomical sums. Finally, in 1982 he could no longer resist and went to Barcelona for £4.2 million, a new world record. It was definitely shaping up as a big year in Diego's life. The World Cup was to be held in Spain, and people's expectations were sky-high. The fact that Argentina was the defending champion seemed to have been forgotten. There was only one player that anyone cared about in the blue and white stripes — Maradona.

The tournament, for both Argentina and Maradona, was a total disaster. In the first group match, Belgium methodically butchered Maradona like a Sunday roast (something to which his shins bore a frightening resemblance after the game). The referee did nothing. Argentina lost 1–0. Victories over Hungary and El Salvador got them to round two, where they were grouped with Italy and Brazil. This was a tough draw for a number of reasons — one of them being Claudio Gentile the Italian defender, one of the most feared and ruthless backs in the game. Gentile tripped, kicked, elbowed and bumped Maradona so consistently and ferociously that he set a new record for fouls by one player on another in a single match (thirty-two in total!). After the game they didn't bother exchanging shirts — Gentile had already torn Maradona's off his back during the first half. Italy won 2–1. Again, the referee did nothing.

In the next match, against Brazil, a bitter and frustrated Maradona lashed out against his opponents. Now the referee did act — and sent him off. He left the field in tears and Argentina lost 3–1.

His next two seasons at Barcelona proved to be very successful (domestic cup winners 1983, European Cup winners and cup champions in 1983), but after the Italians' triumph in the 1982 World Cup all eyes were on Italy's first division. And in 1984 that's where Maradona went, breaking his own world record with a transfer fee of £6.9 million.

Interestingly, though, he didn't follow the 'money trail' to the famous northern Italian clubs like Juventus, AC Milan and Inter Milan. Instead he opted for Napoli, a southern team with no track record in Italian football. This was a significant decision because the industrial north of Italy is much wealthier than the rural south. The fact that Maradona chose the peasants over the landlords instantly made him the most popular resident in Naples. During his eight turbulent seasons with Napoli, Maradona led them to great success (league champions 1987, 1990, cup winners 1987, UEFA cup winners 1989).

Before all that, however, came the thirteenth World Cup finals in 1986. With all eyes turned to Mexico, here, finally, was the perfect stage for Diego Maradona to reveal his genius.

Argentina began in Group 1 with Cup-holders Italy, Bulgaria, and South Korea. Argentina looked shaky. It seemed to be a one-man team, with Maradona doing everything, and doing it unsupported. It was almost as if his team-mates were as much in awe of his abilities as their opponents. They drew 1–1 with Italy due to a piece of Maradona brilliance, and progressed to round two as group leaders.

Here they met the Uruguayans, the undisputed butchers of South American football. Maradona chose this match to unleash his powers. He simply mesmerised his opponents. Although the score was only 1–0, the outcome was never in doubt. The only question was whether Diego's team-mates could stay with him long enough to reach the finals.

In the quarter finals they drew with England. It is this match that is most closely associated with the legend of Diego Maradona, for the best and worst reasons. The game was a real tactical stale-mate: the English swarming in defence; the Argentines looking nervous, unsure of whether to attack. Then Maradona collected the ball outside the English penalty box, played a quick one–two and leapt high above the goalkeeper Shilton to head the opening goal into the net. Great. Only one problem. He headed the ball with his hand. Amidst tumultuous scenes of protest from the English players and rapture from the South American fans, Diego Maradona had done the unforgivable. He had cheated and got away with it.

The next goal was totally different. Collecting the ball in his own half, he spun, accelerated, swerved, dummied, changed pace and direction, accelerated again, dribbled, dummied and then held off a final challenge to beat Shilton again and score perhaps the greatest individual goal in World Cup history. He had run sixty metres, past seven defenders, and side-footed the ball into the net from one metre out. It was a breathtaking moment. Maradona: 2, England: 1.

In the semi-final, Maradona went through the Belgian defence like a wind-up toy gone berserk. Maradona: 2, Belgium: 0. In the final he led Argentina to a 3–2 victory over Germany. The myth was now complete. He *was* the greatest player in the world.

But, oh how quickly things can change. By World Cup 1990 the figure who led Argentina out onto the field bore little resemblance to the pocket-sized dynamo who had seemed so utterly irresistible in Mexico. In his place was a bloated, lame, and in fact rather sad little man. Maradona limped through the tournament on a badly swollen left knee. Argentina somehow survived long enough to make the final, then lost to Germany.

Maradona announced that he no longer wished to play in Italy. The constant attention of the press, the scandals (whether real or invented), and the endless demands of the adoring Napoli fans had taken their toll. Like George Best, he had simply had enough. He just wasn't interested in the grind of training, fitness and matches anymore. However, he still had a contract with Napoli, who said flatly that they would not release him. Then, the first drug scandal broke and Maradona found himself on his way to Seville, Spain.

During the next three years, from 1992 to 1994, Maradona was expelled from football for breach of contract; in court for shooting at newspaper reporters; charged with drug trafficking and being an employer of prostitutes; suspended from football for a positive drug test … etc; etc; etc. It was like a remake of the George Best story word for word. Was it all true? At least some of it probably was.

Without Maradona at the helm, Argentina struggled in the lead up to the World Cup 1994. After being thrashed by Columbia in Buenos Aires, the Argentines were forced to qualify through the repercharge play-off. In this case their opponents were none other than Australia. In a desperate bid to avoid utter public disgrace, the Argentine management approached Maradona to try and coax him out of retirement for one final campaign. Rumours flew through the football world. Yes, he would; no he wouldn't; he's injured; he's too old. Finally, two weeks before the Sydney match, the reports were confirmed: Maradona was in training in an attempt to shed a lot of kilos and get somewhere near match fitness. The guy was thirty-three years old and had played one-and-a-half seasons of real football in four years!

Australia did a more than half-decent job, with a 1–1 draw. Argentina got its goal because of one moment of Maradona genius — a pass hit so perfectly that it virtually compelled the player on the receiving end to run into space with the ball and score with a header. The return match in Argentina was a home-town triumph.

The 1994 finals were held in the USA. In the early games the Argentines blew their opponents away with inspired attacking football. When they came forward they seemed to come from everywhere, and their finishing was absolutely lethal. And at the heart of it all was Maradona, grinning like a maniac and generally having the time of his life. People began to believe that, yes, the miracle might just happen. Then, almost on cue, the big scandal exploded. Maradona was tested for drugs and the result was positive. He was expelled the following day. The impossible dream had been blown apart. It was a bitter disappointment.

Like George Best, Maradona has fought many battles with his addictions, something made all the more difficult for having to do so in public. At the time of writing he is in the best shape he has been in for a decade and is hosting a talk show on Argentine TV. The man is nothing if not resourceful.

GERMANY
2006

World Cup number eighteen began with 205 countries competing for thirty-two places and, 843 qualification matches later, we find ourselves at our third instalment of Sepp's 'super-size me' tournament. The verdict on the thirty-two team format has been, for the most part, very positive. More teams mean more guests at the party which makes it even bigger, richer, and more diverse. And in the spirit of diversity, the 2006 tournament will feature seven debutants: Angola, Ghana, Ivory Coast, Serbia and Montenegro, Togo, Trinidad and Tobago, and the Ukraine.

Only the foolish or seriously delusional try to predict the outcome of a World Cup tournament. It's a bit like the Melbourne Cup in that there are too many starters and too many variables for the serious punter. Take Korea/ Japan 2002 for example. Going into the tournament the fancied teams included Argentina, France, Portugal, Italy, and, as an outsider, Uruguay. Of these, four didn't survive the first round, two didn't win a game, and one couldn't manage a single goal — and they were the defending champions! The pundits' 'players to watch' included Zinedine Zidane, Luis Figo, Gabriel Batistuta, Francesco Totti, and Roy Keane — all great players, but their performances at the last tournament are best described as under-whelming. In the strange case of Roy Keane, he didn't even show up.

One other key factor that makes the result so hard to call in the thirty-two team format is the method of progress to the second round. In the old twenty-four team tournament, the top two teams from six groups plus the four best third place-getters went through to the next round. This meant that you could get away with starting poorly and still have a chance of progressing. Italy in 1982 and Belgium in 1986 are recent examples of good teams who started slowly, but lived to fight another day in the latter part of the tournament. However in Sepp's 'super size me' format there is no margin for error. Start badly and you will almost certainly be eliminated. Every match becomes vital, every result dramatic.

As we head to Germany, the overwhelming favourite is Brazil and on paper it's very hard to argue, but as Johnny Warren loved to remind us, football matches and in particular world cup tournaments are not played on paper. Other teams thought to be worth mentioning are Germany, because they are a) hosts and b) Germany; Italy, because they are Italy; and England for reasons that still remain unclear even at this late stage. Argentina and Holland are both rated highly thanks to a solid year of excellent form. So keeping one eye on the hazards of punditry and the other on the crystal ball, lets take a look at the groups because, let's face it, who can resist?

GROUP A: Germany, Costa Rica, Poland, Ecuador

Germany look to have the measure of this group but they are not without their problems. In Michael Ballack they have a genuine star but without him their game becomes routine and very predictable. They also look to have a few problems with team harmony and stability: coach Jurgen Klinsman's decision to live in the USA for the team's entire preparation has drawn a lot of criticism and the debate over which goalkeeper to play, legendary captain Oliver Kahn or in form Arsenal keeper Jens Lehman, has reached libelous proportions. Costa Rica has been at the two previous finals and this sets a good platform for progress. Paolo Wanchope will, again, be their go-to guy. Ecuador will be appearing at their second tournament in a row, but, playing at sea-level, look to be a little outgunned. Poland are also backing up for their second successive tournament, after a prolonged absence since Mexico 1986, and their form in qualification suggests that they could upset a few apple-carts. Keep an eye on Bayer Leverkusen's dynamic midfielder Jacek Krzynówek

GROUP B: England, Paraguay, Sweden, Trinidad & Tobago

England go into this tournament as they always do: under enormous pressure from their fans and the British media. Following their disappointing exit against Brazil four years ago, they will be desperately keen to do well. They have a truly world class midfield based on Gerrard, Lampard, and Beckham but are they a truly world class team? Who plays up front and the team formation they play in will go a long way to determining their fate. Trinidad and Tobago, spearheaded by Dwight Yorke and Stern John, look outgunned at this level, but then so did Cameroon in 1990 and Senegal in 2002 — if you're good enough to get there, then you're good enough to produce results. Sweden are nothing if not consistent (surprise, surprise) and in Ibramovich, Larsson, and Freddie Ljungberg have players who score regularly in top European competition. They have strong quarter-final claims at least. Paraguay have been threatening to do something big for several world cups but their biggest hurdle remains getting out of the group stage.

GROUP C: Argentina, Ivory Coast, Holland, Serbia & Montenegro

This is a nasty group: as tough as nails and a real contender for 'group of death' status. Twice champions Argentina look very formidable with established stars like Ayala, Crespo, and Messi. In Riquelme they have a player who, if his mind is right, could be the star of the tournament. The Netherlands have been in tremendous form recently and are hungry for success. Well led by coach Marco van Basten, they have an exciting blend of established stars, in van Nistelrooy, van der Sar and captain Phillip Cocu, and upcoming young players. This could be the time to revenge their losses in the finals in '74 and '78. The Ivory Coast can feel unlucky to be drawn in such a tough group and athletic Chelsea striker Drogba and his partner Dindane look to be the key to their success. Serbia and Montenegro qualified strongly and will fear no-one. Their game plan is based in sound defence but in Kezman, Milosevic, and Stankovic they also have genuine goal-scorers and that makes any team dangerous.

GROUP D: Mexico, Angola, Iran, Portugal

Mexico have qualified for the thirteenth time, largely due to an easy qualification path, but even so, last world cup they were strong and continuity is a key element of success. They could certainly do well in the group stage but will need a favourable draw after that. Iran will be underestimated by many because they qualify through Asia — do so at your peril. Thirty-six year old striker Ali Daie could easily do a Roger Milla here. Debutants Angola have done fabulously to get this far. Their 'stars' are captain and former Benfica player Akwa and Manuel and if they can overcome stage fright, then the support from home could well push them through to the next round — but it's a big if. The very talented Portugal was bitterly disappointing four years ago but recovered to be runners-up at Euro 2004. In Renaldo and Deco they possess two of Europe's most dangerous players but as always, the question with Portugal is never talent but temperament — if that's right, then look out.

GROUP E: Italy, Ghana, USA, Czech Republic

Italy, Italy, Italy — sixteen appearances and three times champions, they are overdue for a victory lap. Close in '90, closer in '94, and closer still in '98, they must be prepared to go forward or risk a frustrating exit like in 2002. So much comes down to coach Lippi and whether he can harness the talent at his disposal and combine it into a fluid unit. The early signs are positive, such as their humiliation of the hosts in March 2006. The biggest question about Ghana is why they took so long to get here. Traditionally one of the powerhouses of African football and with players of the caliber of Appiah, Chelsea's Michael Essien and Udinese's Muntari, they could do anything. The US shocked everyone four years ago with the strength of their performance and we can expect more of the same from a team that plays well for one another. In McBride and Beasley they have enough bang to scare a few ducks off the pond. The Czech Republic could be the real sleepers of this tournament. Well organized in defense and exciting in attack, they are good enough to stretch anyone. The fitness of keeper Chech and attacking midfielder Nedved are critical to their chances.

GROUP F: Brazil, Croatia, Australia, Japan

It's enough to make you sick, isn't it. Thirty-two bloody years and we get Brazil. Thank you very much. And this team is probably more favoured to win than any Brazilian team in history. The pressure is enormous and thank god we're not playing them first. Players to watch? That's easy — all of them: Ronaldhino, Kaka, Juninho, Robinho, Adriano … enough already. They could easily establish themselves as one of the greatest teams in history but talent alone doesn't guarantee success, just ask Hungary in '54, Holland in '74, Brazil in '50, '82, and '86, France in '82 and '86. You get the picture. Poor Croatia qualified undefeated but have the misfortune to meet them first up and it will make or break the Croatian's tournament — an unlikely victory and they will be unstoppable, a thrashing and they will struggle to recover. Unlike the swashbuckling team of '98 with it's brilliant attack, this year's team is based on a rock-solid defence and so much will depend on

their main man up front, Dado Prso. Australia — finally, how sweet
it is. The Aussies will fear no-one and in Hiddink have a genuine
master coach. Injuries and yellow cards are their major threat as
the squad is light on for depth in key positions (e.g. central defense
and wide attack) and an injury to Harry Kewell would severely
stretch the squad. Some players are not getting regular match time
in Europe and this is a worry, but having said that, key players
Viduka, Aloisi, Cahill, Kewell, and Bresciano are all in form and
scoring goals in the major leagues. These guys have the capability
to win us one and possibly two games in this group. Bring it on!
Japan are Asian champions but seem strangely under-confident
about their chances, despite going into the finals for the third time
in a row. Let's hope they're right. Their key players are Nakata,
Nakamura, and Shinji Ono.

GROUP G: France, Switzerland, South Korea, Togo

The French are a shadow of the great teams of the 1998–2000 era
but in Zidane and Henry they still have a treasure chest of potential — just like in the 2002 finals when they were frankly appalling.
These two guys need to fire and the rest of the team just needs to
do the opposite of what it did in 2002, and if they do, then look
out because these guys are using technology. For a country whose
national sport is banking, the Swiss do all right. They will look to
the teamwork thing to get their results and are a good bet for the
second round. South Korea blew everyone away with their semi-
final berth in 2002 but this time, away from home and without
Hiddink, they'll find it a lot harder. Togo will probably be everybody's second team along with Angola. Their key man is Adebayor
and their main problems will be stage fright and not getting red-
carded for over-the-top tackling — a perennial problem for most
African nations that have made it to previous tournaments.

GROUP H: Spain, Ukraine, Tunisia, Saudi Arabia

Spain could well be the greatest under-achievers in the history of world cup football. As usual they boast a formidable roster and a rich culture — as they have on their eleven previous appearances. Frankly, I can't see this tournament being much different to previous ones for them. Ukraine, who like to play with three strikers, can be really lethal but all will depend on Shevchenko and that is a heavy load to carry on the biggest stage in the world (just think of Ballack in'98). Tunisia are coached by highly motivated Frenchman Lemerre, who oversaw the disastrous French campaign in 2002 — he has a lot to prove. Tunisia are really useful and could surprise, in much the same way as the USA did four years ago. Saudia Arabia will be making their fourth appearance at the big show and provided they start better than the 8–0 loss they copped first-up four years ago, they could make the next round. Group H looks like a two horse race, so their match with Ukraine will be vital.